Wild
FOOD PLANTS OF
Hawai'i
SUNNY SAVAGE

DEDICATION

To my three boys, who are with me always and forever.

ACKNOWLEDGMENTS

I must acknowledge the plants, who have become teachers and allies and healers along my path. In fact, let us acknowledge the tree whose life was cut short to make this book, or elements dug up from deep in the earth to make and power your computer, so that we may share knowledge and work towards evolving our consciousness. I must acknowledge my Mom, who has a bottomless well of love from which she has cloaked me in my whole life long. This book was an absolute labor of love that wouldn't have been possible without the support of my husband Ryan, who watched a whole lot of baby and did a whole lot of dishes, to get us through. Mahalo nui to Nancy Bouwsma for manuscript edits and Hunter Haskins for helping with the bibliography. A big shout out to Forest and Kim Starr from Starr Environmental, who graciously provided many of the images in this book, as well as maps for my TedxMaui 2014 talk. The beautiful Cadence Feely of Cadencia Photography, who shot many of the food photographs in my wild kitchen, Sue Hudelson Photography, John Kallas of Wild Food Adventures, Karen Raczewski Monger of The 3 Foragers, David Bruce Leonard, Winona LaDuke, Paula Fuga, and Vince Dodge for their photos and support. And finally, to the wild cast of characters who are into this wild food thing…keep shining your light.

TABLE OF CONTENTS

© 96
VAREZ/CI

Menu

DRINKS

Lychee & Red Hibiscus Martini

Orange & Wild Bitters Fizz

PUPU

Elderflower Tempura

Wild Ginger & Lemongrass Dipping Sauce

SOUP

Coconut Cream of Wild Amaranth

MAIN

Venison Stuffed with Wild Herbs and Poha Chutney
served with Cats Ear Flower Fronds &
Wild Pine-Infused Ulu Salad

DESSERT

Wild Beach Almond Coconut Ice Cream

Feral Guava Sauce

FERAL FRAPPE

Wildcrafted Coffee

Kiawe & Wild Allspice Syrup

AS WE BEGIN THIS MEAL WITH GRACE
LET US BECOME AWARE OF THE MEMORY
CARRIED INSIDE THE FOOD BEFORE US:
THE QUIVER OF THE SEED
AWAKENING IN THE EARTH,
UNFOLDING IN THE TRUST OF ROOTS
AND SLENDER STEMS OF GROWTH,
ON ITS VOYAGE TOWARD HARVEST,
THE KISS OF RAIN AND SURGE OF SUN;
THE INNOCENCE OF ANIMAL SOUL
THAT NEVER SPOKE A WORD,
NOURISHED BY THE EARTH
TO BECOME TODAY OUR FOOD;
THE WORK OF ALL THE STRANGERS
WHOSE HANDS PREPARED IT,
THE PRIVILEGE OF WEALTH AND HEALTH
THAT ENABLES US TO FEAST AND CELEBRATE.

-John O'Donohue
To Bless the Space Between Us

© 1996
VAREZ/CI

EXTREME FORAGING

WILD FOOD MANIFESTO

This is an invitation to unwrap the gift of wild foods. They are growing in your own backyard, at the beach, on farms, and in our forests. Do you see them? Our ancestors could, and you will too. Utilize this wild card, which you might not have even thought was in the game, to assist your DNA in expressing the best of your genetic traits. This is a call to action, a return to wild health by eating *one wild food every day*.

A wise person once told me to put on a magic backpack and imagine myself pulling out a slingshot to remove outdated concepts. It works, and I'd like to gift you your own magic backpack now. Imagine it as being full of many wonderful things, but you're going to take that slingshot out and shoot the concept of a weed into a gigantic black hole. Let it be transmuted, recycled, or whatever the heck happens in those places. Open yourself to this curious new world free of weeds, which is full of medicinal plants, beautiful plants, and those we're even lucky enough to be able to eat. *Hawai'i nei* is a forager's paradise, with mountaintop to ocean foraging. This book is just the beginning of your journey, a diving board from which to jump out and into the wilds of Hawai'i.

Once you are out in the wilds of Hawai'i, be 100% sure of identification before you ever eat a wild plant. Respect the plants enough to know who they are. Madagascar fireweed (*Senecio madagascariensis*) is full of pyrrolizidine alkaloids, many of which are toxic to humans. The taste would be so bad you wouldn't be able to choke it down, but I have seen many people confuse its identity with edible plants like cat's ear (*Hypochaeris radicata*) and oriental hawksbeard (*Youngia japonica*). Seek out people who know about plants and who are willing to share that knowledge with you. A forager's paradise awaits.

Eating wild foods is nothing new. Indigenous people around the world still identify and utilize a large diversity of wild foods, with an average of 120 wild species used per cultural group (1). This knowledge has often been passed through multiple generations, and continues in both industrialized and developing countries. Learning about wild food plant identification, the stories and myths they are a part of, physically getting outside and harvesting wild foods, preparing them to eat, sharing that food with others while you tell your tales of how it was discovered, or the adventure had in getting there, is all part of the complex and rich gift that wild foods are. Delight in the newness of eating *one wild food every day*, along with remembrance for all those that have kept this practice alive.

Wild foods alone are not going to feed everyone on earth, but everyone on earth could be eating wild foods. Our industrialized society has moved away from many of the strong flavors found in wild food plants, but those flavors were once coveted by all of our ancestors for their prophylactic qualities, having both powerful medicinal and preventative health qualities. Micronutrient deficiencies now rank among the top twenty risk factors for morbidity and impaired quality of life worldwide, and occur in both high and low income countries (2). Imagine yourself going to the doctor and saying, "I'm eating a diversity of unprocessed industrial-agriculture-free foods in my diet, and eat at least *one wild food every day*."

Quality, not quantity, is where our wild foods shine. You don't need to be out harvesting huge amounts of them, as just adding small amounts really does make a difference. Wild foods are exceptional sources of micronutrients (vitamins and minerals), phytochemicals, allelochemicals, fiber, and a list of other things we don't even know about yet. They are superstars in the nutrition world, and the power of eating small amounts was highlighted in a recent study by Dr. Bronwen Powell *et al.*, who found that participants met over 30% of their daily vitamin A requirements, 20% of their vitamin C, and 19% of their iron from eating just 2% of their daily calories in wild foods (3). Only 2 percent!

What will be on our dinner plates in 2050? The inherent resilience of wild species in adapting to climate change means they could increasingly be a buffer against food security issues. Climate watchers are expecting increased droughts here in Hawai'i during the next 50 years, so in addition to being free, wild foods do not require water for irrigation. With over 10% of our state population living below the poverty level, a much higher level of working poor, and inflation not even addressing increasing food costs on the islands, wild foods just might be at the beach barbecue of 2050. Free, nutritious, widely available…what's not to love?

MY STORY

My mother says that when I entered this world the forest was carpeted with a blanket of blooming trillium. The maple syrup harvest had just finished, and the homestead my parents had cleared in the thick forest of the Smoky Hills of northern Minnesota buzzed with new spring life. Those early years were spent without running water or electricity, where we grew

food in large gardens and raised pigs. Wild berries and honeysuckle flowers provided enchantment and food. I was often seen running naked with cowboy boots and flowers in my hair, the forest bearing witness to that wild freedom. I was gifted with back-to-the-land parents who provided a fertile area from which to grow, and have been blessed with early memories of being loved.

I come from a long line of adventurers. My father was a physics and calculus teacher who went on great adventures of the mind. At times I felt as if he were one of the few who actually touched the edges of the universe. Nearly fluent in 5 languages, he was a renaissance man who sparked a feeling in me that anything was possible. His father was also a great adventurer, and a warrior, and I remember him telling animated stories of eating monkey brains in Africa and jumping out of planes in Germany. He was a Harvard graduate, who became a foreign diplomat and CIA operative, and brought their large family to live in Algeria, the Philippines and Madagascar. He ate raw poison ivy leaves every spring as a tonic, and was always curious about the wild foods I shared with him.

Tales of our genealogy were often told, but it was the story of my ancestor Thomas Savage that reached out through the halls of time to grab me and so intimately shape my destiny. You see Thomas was an adventurer as well, and at 13 he left Europe and traveled to the New World. It was 1607 and young Thomas was on the second boat that landed in what is now known as Jamestown. Shortly after arriving, he was involved in a political exchange that placed him in the home of Chief Powhatan. Young Savage and the Chief got along well, as well as the Chief's famous daughter Pocahontas. Thomas Savage became a translator and negotiator as the old world and the new world danced into a new way of being. He died at an early age, and I feel there is work he guides me to do.

And what of the women? My mothers line has been connected to farming the land for so long that its history simply became the sound of the earth herself. A circle of Norwegian, French, Irish, German, Polish, and Maltese women are all part of my story. If we should meet on the great battlefields of life, this is from where I rise up.

At 18 I left to work in the kitchen of a research station in Antarctica for a year. Eating stir-fried penguin got really old. Just kidding! A year of eating highly processed canned

and frozen foods in the frozen south had turned my attention to the importance of good food. I knew my life path involved wild foods when I came home and read in some of my moms herbal medicine books that several of the medicinal plants were also edible. I jumped off a springboard and dove into my adult life with a passion for wild foods.

After graduating with a Bachelor's of Science in Dietetics from St. Catherine University, I returned home looking for work. But a nose ring made it difficult to find a job in my small town. A short world away was Winona LaDuke on the White Earth Reservation. I had heard of her work starting the White Earth Land Recovery Project and Honor the Earth, and figured I would see if there was some way I could become involved. She laughed, said she had seen the editorial I wrote to the local paper stating my frustration with the community's conservative attitudes about a nose ring, and hired me as a nutritionist. Although it was short-lived, it was my first job related to wild foods.

My time in White Earth opened those young eyes to the agrochemical and biotech companies' desecration of Mother Earth. Fueled with the idealism of youth, which I'm happy to say I've never lost, I moved to Flagstaff, AZ to attend Northern Arizona University. A professor encouraged me to apply for a summer internship at the Center for Food Safety in Washington D.C., and I spent a summer rallying up chef signatures to petition the feds to keep GMO salmon out of our oceans. I returned to Arizona and moved onto the Navajo Reservation with my Dineh boyfriend, becoming pregnant with my first son Saelyn.

Life excludes no one of challenges, and I found myself as a single mom for the next 5 years. I landed a job working full time at the White Earth Tribal and Community College and getting my Masters of Science in Nutrition Education from the Rosalind Franklin University of Medicine and Science. It was during that time the Local Food Challenge was born, where seven of us joined in solidarity to eat foods grown within 250 miles of where we lived for one year. I got into video during this time and made a small documentary about our experiences living the Local Food Challenge, which aired on our local public television station and at the Northern Lights Indigenous Film Festival. The Wild Food Summit, an annual gathering of wild foodies I helped co-found, was also birthed during this time. Wild and local just felt right.

keep i

Help Minnesota Anishinaabeg stop the genetic
contamination of sacred manoomin.

Protect our state grain and cultural heritage. Keep genetically engineered wild rice out of Minnesota. ■ Painting - *Nenaboozho and Nookomis Rising* by Rabbett J.

KEEP IT WILD
Don't Change Wild Rice | Gego Aanjitooken Manoomin

White Earth Land Recovery Project's campaign to stop the genetic engineering of wild rice.
Photo Courtesy of White Earth Land Recovery Project

Hot on the Trail with Sunny Savage came to be when a producer saw one of the wild food YouTube videos I'd made while living in Topanga Canyon, CA. Within 2 weeks I had a signed contract and was to spend nearly a year living in an RV, traveling to filming locations in 17 states across America. During a trip to film our episodes in Hawai'i, I fell in love with my charming innkeeper. We like to joke that I checked in and never checked out. We were married and immediately took off for a 3-year honeymoon, sailing over 6,000 miles in the Caribbean. We put our energy into filming a docudrama about the skills our youth will need to thrive in a rapidly changing future. We returned home and had a son 9 months later!

Filming the wild mustard episode of Hot on the Trail with Sunny Savage.

Cleaning the spreader tips while living aboard the Saelyn Grima.

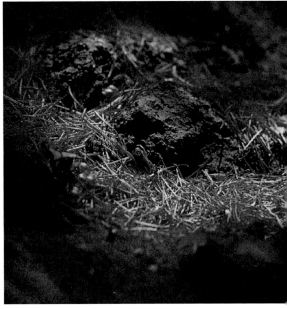

Ohi'a 'ai (Syzygium malaccense) was blooming when my son Zeb was born. Its neon pink flower petals and mountain apples are edible.

I Ola No Ke Kino

I ola no ke kino

I ka mā'ona no ka 'ōpū

I mā'ona no ka 'ōpū

Me ke aloha o ka makua

E pū pa'akai kākou

Me ka mahalo

Ua loa'a ho'i iā kākou

Ka 'ai a me ke aloha

May the body live

Because the stomach is full

May the stomach be full

With love of the parent

Let us share salt

With thanks

That all we have

At Savage Farms, my family's version of a wild farm, we work on Maui's north shore to regenerate the land and grow food. The wild food plants that move through our permaculture-inspired agroforestry system are welcomed. It is from this home, perched on a cliff in the jungle, that my story continues.

THE HARVEST

Wild food knowledge is an evolving continuum, with experience at its heart. Experience is earned, something no one can take away from you, and it is not something a book or internet search can provide. Once you are 100% sure of your identification, you will find yourself with an opportunity to harvest an abundance of food at times. In Hawai'i we have the good fortune of being able to eat fresh food year-round, unlike the years of my life spent in northern Minnesota where most harvesting was limited to less than half of the year. Canning, fermenting, freezing, drying, cooking with stones, and cooking within the earth, like the Hawaiian imu, are important skills to know no matter where home may be.

Now that you have harvested food, what are you going to do with it? This photo shows a combination of over 20 different wild and cultivated foods harvested at Savage Farms.

TOOLS OF THE TRADE

Just accept the fact that you've gotten a new hobby, with a new set of tools. In addition to what you see here, like the dehydrator, I also often utilize tarps, fruit pickers, headlamps, scissors, a loupe, solar oven, bags and containers of all sorts, and lots of jars.

THERE'S A MAGIC THAT HAPPENS *in each person's kitchen as earth,*
air, fire, water and 'the mystery' come together in unique ways. This book doesn't have a lot of
recipes, as in this day and age I find that recipes skew people's ideas on what and how they can cook.
There's nothing like finding a good recipe, for sure, but don't let it limit you. Utilize as much of the
harvest as you can, and keep experimenting through the failures.

PLATE 1.

The majority of people around the planet are now eating plain processed carbohydrates, with not much else added to them.

PLATE 2.

Try adding just one wild food to what you're already eating.

3.

4.

5.

IF YOU WANT TO BE BEAUTIFUL,

then you need to eat beautiful.
Plain noodles are transformed
with wild ingredients.

3. Beach Almonds

4. Popolo Berries

5. Red Hibiscus

6. Wild Greens Powder

7. Wild Edible Flowers

6.

7.

ETHICS OF WILDCRAFTING

There was this day, when I was about 20 years old and living in northern Minnesota, where the forest was absolutely buzzing with life. I was hot on the trail of some wild foods, and my jaw nearly dropped when I spotted a large stand of bee balm *(Monarda fistulosa)*, a plant I had been excitedly trying to locate for some time. Overcome with enthusiasm, I harvested large basketfuls. I woke up the next morning and looked at the basketfuls with deep feelings of panic and regret. I had seriously overharvested and learned a very important and painful lesson; don't take more than you're going to use. My cousin Ila Hatter taught me the following, a general guideline for right relationship with the plants:

Rule of Four

1. Pass by the first plant so that it can go to seed.

2. Pass by the second plant so that the animals, insects, and fungi can coexist with it.

3. Pass by the third plant so that it is available for a brother or sister in need.

4. You are now invited to harvest.

The Ethics of Wildcrafting command us to use respect. I love the definition of respect "to look again". Have you identified, with 100% certainty, the plant you would like to harvest? Have you asked for permission to harvest? Is the area free of herbicides, pesticides, fungicides, and chemical fertilizers? Sometimes you will need to connect with an area for several years before you have a real understanding of how to harvest in a sustainable and safe way. This is the wealth of our biodiversity we're talking about, so step up and honor our lovely wild foods through right relationship.

Take the time to tune into your environment. Put the cell phone away and put your hand on the earth. Do images come to mind? Feelings? What does your intuition tell you? What are the sounds and smells? I know it sounds like some kind of New Age wish wash, but the reality is that the earth is alive and if you think that the natural world is not in communication with you, then you are a bit outdated in your mental concepts. Developing relationships with plants requires a willingness to be open to the many modalities by which a plant might communicate.

Having spent many years living on or near Indian Reservations, I was taught to give tobacco as a gift for plants that would be harvested. Here in Hawai'i, I typically take a moment to think beautiful thoughts, sing a song, or pule, which is the Hawaiian word for prayer, before harvesting a plant. Gift giving is very personal, and there are many ways it can be done, but by making this gesture you are signaling your intention to the plant and yourself.

It is our sacred responsibility to caretake the earth. Malama da 'aina!

Over and over again I have witnessed the wonderment in a child's eyes as a wild green is plucked from the ground and eaten. Children naturally follow suit if a trusted adult gives the nod of approval, and in short order they are eating liberally of these newfound treasures. Bring them home, cook them, and try to get them to eat their vegetables…well that is a different story altogether! For some reason there's a palpable magic to eating directly from nature's wild garden. With childlike pleasure wild greens are the most sought-after addition to my wild diet.

The following pages cover some of my favorite wild greens and vegetables, but there are so many more that have graced my table here on Maui. Green papaya (*Carica papaya*), although widely cultivated, is oftentimes growing wild and makes for an easily foraged vegetable. I like to shred it into green salad, cooked and chilled for cold salads, or boiled in soups. Similar in texture is the oftentimes feral chayote squash (*Sechium edule*). Called pipinola in Hawaiian, it has gone feral in many places on Maui and both the vine tips and squash provide an abundant and delicious food source. Rumors of ivy gourd (*Coccinia grandis*) and its delicious greens come from foraging friends on Oahu, where it has escaped cultivation. Peppergrass (*Lepidium spp.*) is an abundant little herb whose spicy leaves, along with black mustard (*Brassica nigra*), nasturtium greens (*Tropaeolum majus*), and watercress greens (*Nasturtium officinale*) provide a diversity of spicy wild greens. Prickly pear (*Opuntia spp.*) has thick pads that make for a substantial and interesting vegetable once the spines and glochids are removed. I've kept my son busy harvesting the newly emerging grass tips of wandering jew (*Tradescantia fluminensis*), known as honohono grass in Hawaiian, which get cooked into things like fritatta's at my house. Common plantain (*Plantago major*) is found in abundance, of whose seeds and leaves can be eaten. Australian Tree Fern (*Cyathea cooperi)* is rumored to have an edible inner core, which could potentially be a fabulous way of eating this invasive that is taking over on Kaua'i. Young bamboo shoots and pohole fern (*Diplazium esculentum and D. sandwichianum*) are more widely recognized as edible. *Erechtites valerianifolia's* young greens and stem, along with small to medium-sized False Awa (*Piper auritum*) leaves are somewhat controversial, but have become favorites in our household. Dandelions (*Taraxacum officinale)*, chickweed (*Stellaria media*), and the list goes on. Eat your wild greens I say…eat your wild greens!

EATING A DIVERSITY OF WILD GREENS
IS DEEPLY NOURISHING.

CAT'S EAR

(Hypochaeris radicata)

Cat's Ear leaf, unopened flower bud, and flower.

Native to Eurasia, this plant has now naturalized on Ni`ihau, Kaua`i, O`ahu, Moloka`i, Lana`i, Maui, Kaho`olawe, and Hawai`i. We begin our journey with a wild plant that should be fairly easy to find, no matter which island you live on.

When I moved to Maui I began the search for one of my old wild food allies called dandelion (*Taraxacum officinale*). I couldn't believe how hard it was to find dandelion, and saw that it was far outnumbered by the prolific cat's ear. Cat's ear is oftentimes called false dandelion, and although they are two different plants, they can be used in much the same way.

Cat's Ear is found in abundance on the slopes of Haleakala.

The entire plant is edible, and just like dandelion it is bitter. Bitter flavors can be masked by the addition of fat or sweet flavors. With the introduction of highly processed foods, many people have now lost their taste for bitters, but if you can learn to like beer you can learn to like bitter greens. Try making an herbal vinegar with cat's ear. By chopping up the washed roots, leaves, stems and flowers of this highly invasive plant to our sensitive Haleakala grasslands, we are doing our part to bring the system back in balance. The chopped cat's ear is packed into a jar, with a clove of garlic, and covered with apple cider vinegar or locally brewed vinegar. Be sure to seal it with a non-metal lid to avoid corrosion. Let this sit for 4-6 weeks, although you can begin to use it immediately, keeping it out of the sun and shaking occasionally. The plant material is strained out when you achieve the flavor you want, and you have a fine herbal vinegar that can be used liberally in your salads, on bean soups, when cooking meats, or however your culinary imagination sees fit. The *Asian Pacific Journal of Tropical Biomedicine* recently published a study showing that the leaves and roots are an outstanding source of antioxidants (4), and my intuition tells me that its flowers must contain a plethora of phytonutrients as well.

Another way of eating cat's ear I learned from my foraging friend John Kallas, who lives in the Pacific Northwest where the plant also grows prolifically. Unopened flower stalks can be snapped off where tender and steamed or sautéed for an interesting vegetable. You can see a photo of these on the next page.

Cat's ear grows in a basal rosette.

Cat's ear flower stalks. Photo Courtesy of John Kallas, Wild Food Adventures

FERAL FENNEL

(Foeniculum vulgare)

This is my son Saelyn's favorite wild green. He liberally tears off handfuls of the leaves, packing them into his mouth as fast as he can, and has been doing so since he was 4 years old. We first became introduced to this plant while living in Topanga Canyon, CA.

I look forward to spending time on the slopes of Haleakala, teaching it to my newborn son Zeb as he grows, but

Newly emerging feral fennel frond.

in some ways he already knows quite a bit about it. Besides the fact that children learn by watching us, and he has already witnessed mom harvesting a lot of it, this plant was an incredible ally while I was pregnant with him. Long known for its ability to get rid of gas and promote digestion, I turned to it often to combat painful indigestion during pregnancy. Its seeds hold the most powerful punch in regards to medicinal use, see page 108 for more about wild fennel seeds.

Native to the Mediterranean, it is now found on the islands of Kaua'i, Oahu, Maui, Lana'i, and Hawai'i. If you're into botany it can be described as having pinnately decompound leaves with filiform ultimate divisions and broadly sheathing petioles! Look for its feathery leaves up in the Kula area on Maui, and look for the fleshy fronds, shown in the photo above, which can be pulled or cut off at their base to fill your foraging basket with a delicious wild vegetable. Try sautéing the fronds with some venison sausage, onion, and garlic. Serve with kalo for a delicious meal. Wild fennel goes well with many local seafoods and sea vegetables. Blanched fronds and greens are an essential part of Sicily's famed *pasta con sarde*. Save the water you used to blanch them and use it to cook something else, like sweet potatoes or to drink as a tea. Are you a barbeque fanatic?

Feral Fennel Habitat. Photo Courtesy Forest & Kim Starr

Try putting some dried fennel stalks on the coals and use the smoke to flavor your food as it cooks. Or maybe you like fermented foods and want to turn the fronds into a pickle that could be added to ulu salad. I also love adding it to herb butter, see page 30.

Feral fennel is a great source of micronutrients like potassium, calcium, magnesium, iron, phosphorous, and zinc (5). Free radical scavenging activity, which is one of the ways scientists measure health promoting activity, has shown higher in wild fennel than in cultivated, but both are worthy additions to your diet (6).

EXPERIMENT WITH THE FEATHERY
LEAVES OF FERAL FENNEL.

HERB BUTTER

1 stick of unsalted butter, softened

1 Tbsp feral fennel, minced

1 Tbsp feral parsley, minced

1 tsp garlic, smashed and minced

Hawaiian sea salt to taste

Mix ingredients. Refrigerate.

FERAL PARSLEY

(Petroselinum crispum)

Now found on Kaui'i, Oahu, Maui, and Hawai'i, this flat-leaved variety has escaped cultivation and found its way onto our wild dinner plates in Hawai'i. This plant has been in use for a few thousand years.

Look for its toothed or lobed leaves, along with its distinctive flower umbels shown in the photo below, and characteristic smell when crushed.

Once you find it don't just add a sprig to your plate for garnish. This nutritious herb should be used liberally, as it packs a powerful punch with vitamin K, vitamin C, vitamin A, iron and folic acid all weighing in heavily. It is high in antioxidants and flavonoids, and is also thought to increase the benefits of other antioxidants (7). Add it to some wild chicken eggs for breakfast, tabouleh, or jackfruit seed bean dip. Liberally add it to your salads, or add it to the herb butter shown on the previous page. Just eat it! Although it's best to use fresh, it can be dried and used later. If you begin to be interested in using the seeds or roots, do so in much smaller quantity, especially if you are pregnant or breastfeeding.

Umbrella-shaped flowers of feral parsley.

GOTU KOLA

(Centella asiatica)

"two leaves a day keeps old age away"

Known as pohe kula in Hawaiian, this sturdy little plant has long been known as the longevity herb.

Holding the imagination of storytellers for years, it's said that there were Tai Chi masters in China

Photo Courtesy Forest & Kim Starr

who lived over 200 years due to ingesting it daily. And the plant has continued its use through the ages, being confirmed by modern science to have cognitive-enhancing effects (8). It is small and creeping, with fan-shaped leaves, and is typically found in areas where the earth is moist.

Gotu kola is a perennial evergreen with kidney shaped leaves.

Although I mostly eat its leaves, it has been shown that the roots also contain the powerful phenolic compounds giving it such strong antioxidant powers (9). If you find yourself needing to eradicate this somewhat invasive plant then you will need to remove its roots, so why let them go to waste? This is not a plant that I eat in large quantity, but I do eat it regularly. It has a strong flavor, similar to carrot tops, and is a member of the Apiaceae Family. Think of it more as an herb, to be used for good health and flavor, rather than the bulk of your diet.

Gotu kola chiffonade.

A chiffonade is a chopping technique where you roll the leaves and then thinly slice them from the side. This is a great way to balance, or dilute, the strong flavor of gotu kola. In fact, many greens with powerful flavors are taken from substandard fare into deliciousness when treated this way. Try mixing your gotu kola chiffonade with grated coconut, minced onion, garlic, ginger, chilis, lime juice, and salt. Or try putting it in tabouleh, or added to miso soup.

Gotu kola juice with tamarind and kaffir lime syrup.

MALLOW

(Malva neglecta & M. parviflora)

For those living on Maui, have you ever taken a drive on Omaopio Road during the rainy season and noticed this one? That road, full of farms, has choke mallow and most farmers just shake their head and laugh when I ask to harvest it from their fields. The entire plant can be utilized for food and medicine, but it is the leaves that are harvested in quantity quickly. By the time you get home they will have gone limp, but no worries because not all has been lost. This is the primary green that I dehydrate and grind up into a wild green superfood powder. Yes, those fresh greens can be put into stews or sautés, but my primary use for them is powdered.

Photo Courtesy of Forest & Kim Starr

Why? Because their mucilaginous qualities make for an absolutely delightful thickener. Use the powder to thicken soups and sauces, or add to smoothies or in eggs to make green eggs and ham.

Mallow grows profusely during the winter rains.

WILD GREENS SUPERFOOD POWDER

A hot car with windows rolled up has always been known to dry plants, and ovens on low can work, but the best way to preserve the nutrients found in wild greens is to use a dehydrator at a low temperature until the moisture has been removed. Those fully dried leaves are then put into a blender, or some device that can pulverize them. Put your wild greens superfood powder into a jar with a tight-fitting lid and use liberally for good nutritional measure.

The seedpods of mallow make for a curious little vegetable. They have been called cheeses and discs, and make perfect frisbees for the fairies. These little wheels of fortune take quite some time to harvest in quantity, so bring some friends. I consider them as a special occasion food, to mark the great turning of the wheel, the balance of the circle, and the symbolism of the seed. The following recipe celebrates that turn in our annual orbit around the sun where we are at our darkest point and then we tip the tide and return to the light. Rainy winter weather during the *makahiki*, which is the Hawaiian New Year and time of peace, comes near the winter solstice and the fields and forests are flush with food.

WINTER SOLSTICE

Return of the Light Celebration Recipe

¼ cup mallow seed wheels

1 Tbsp coconut oil

½ cup macadamia nuts

1 tsp curry powder

salt

flowers for garnish

Put macadamia nuts and mallow seed wheels in a skillet and toast them until done to your liking. Add coconut oil, then curry powder once oil is heated, and stir mix on medium high heat for another minute. Remove from heat, add salt, and mix well. Garnish with wild edible flowers.

We are blessed with coconut oil and macadamia nuts, whose fat keeps us warm when watching the Pleiades rise on cool winter evenings. The ʻolena, known as turmeric in English, turns the nuts and seeds a golden yellow, symbolizing the return of the light.

NEW ZEALAND SPINACH

(Tetragonia tetragonioides)

Photo Courtesy of Forest & Kim Starr

This is one delicious green! It has always fascinated me that although it is predominantly found along the seashore, I find it growing up to 4,000 ft in upper Kula. Reported on all of our major islands, except Kaho'olawe and Ni'hau, it is well adapted to growing in salty conditions (10). I have seen this plant growing wild all over in its native New Zealand and Australia. It was one of the few wild plants that were acceptable to the Europeans, and even gained some recognition in the early 19th century as a summer spinach in Britain and America.

Its triangular, pointed, fleshy leaves are a delight to find when tender and succulent. As with all plants you should have a discerning eye when harvesting wild foods. Your eyes can see where the tender new growth of a plant is and you will naturally be attracted to those vital parts. If you find something that doesn't look good, don't eat it! Not related to spinach botanically, it can be used in many of the same ways. I never eat it raw, and luckily it actually holds up better than spinach when cooked. Blanch greens in boiling water for a minute, dumping out the cooking water, and then rinsing in cold water. Some people blanch them twice if the flavor is strong, or if they're concerned about oxalates. This is your starting point, and you can now add them to anything where you normally would have used spinach. If you have an abundance, then freeze it after it has been blanched and cooled. Maybe you want to try it sautéed with wild pepiou mushrooms (*Auricularia cornea, A. polytricha, & A. tenuis*), ginger and garlic, and stuffed into dumplings. Maybe mixed with taro leaf in your next batch of laulau, or stewed in coconut milk over some sweet potatoes. Wherever New Zealand Spinach ends up, I think you will be quite delighted with this delicious cooked wild green.

ORIENTAL HAWKSBEARD

(Youngia japonica)

Native to southeastern Asia, this plant has now naturalized on nearly all inhabited islands. It is an absolute delight to have around, and it is probably the green I eat most during the rainy season because it grows so prolifically in my own Haiku backyard. The leaves grow in a loose basal rosette, and their oblanceolate shape is lobed to varying degrees. Sometimes I find its leaf edges having a dark brown or black color to them, and the leaves are typically no larger than 6" long by 3" wide.

Oriental hawksbeard is an abundant wild green that is typically found during the rainy season.

They are mild in flavor and can be easily added raw in salads or sandwiches. Although I wouldn't boil them for any length of time, they can be added at the end of cooking to add a wild greens twist.

OXALIS SPP.

(Oxalis debilis var. corymbosa & O. corniculata)

Can you imagine a food so lovely as to be in the shape of a heart? Nearly everyone calls this plant clover, but if you look closely you will be able to tell it is something quite different when you see the hearts. This small and unassuming little plant is one of the most common wild edible plants found around the globe, and has been a globetrotter for so long, that its origins remain a mystery. Intuitively known as edible by children across the planet, it is delightfully sour and all parts above ground can be eaten, including the cylindrical seed capsules.

Photo Courtesy Forest & Kim Starr

It is found on all of our inhabited Hawaiian Islands, so keep your eyes peeled low to the ground and once you have it locked into memory you will notice its ubiquitous presence. The species with yellow flowers (*O. corniculata*) is much more common, and provides some vitamin C and iron (11). The pink species (*O. debilis var. corymbosa*) can grow to a much larger size and are a nice source of magnesium (12).

Oxalis debilis can get quite large!

What a delight to be served a dish where someone has taken the time to put their energy into separating the leaflets into hearts. This kind of thing calls for the sound of the 'ukeke and a lei for your lover. In the future we just may see restaurants around the island demanding this one to garnish dishes on Valentine's Day.

Many call this a weed, but we are utilizing a sling shot from our
that word into a gigantic black hole. This plant is a high quality
ng a nutritional superstar, has a tenacity for life that outdoes
akulikuli kula in Hawaiian, and is found anywhere there are
The photos below show how it grows in my garden beds.
ad greens for us, instead I have a virtual forest of purslane.
g in my richly fertilized garden beds, the plant is also promising in
that is does well in the face of increasing salt buildup in our farmlands. Salty soil presents
challenging growing conditions for most cultivated plants, but purslane persists (13).

Harvest purslane when it is vibrant and succulent. You can keep eating it while it flowers, along with its little seedpods that spill out black seeds. Anything that looks tender and healthy is edible. I see many people throw away its crunchy stems, but they are also a delicious vegetable and provide much protection to our DNA from the onslaught of damages brought by modern-day life (108). This plant has a long list of nutrients, with omega-3 fatty acids being the most widely talked about. It is truly bursting with nutrients like beta-carotene, and recent research continues to secure its place among nutritional superstars with flavonoids, calcium, vitamin E, vitamin C, calcium, zinc and more (14, 15).

One of my favorite ways of using purslane is to make it into something similar to a french onion soup. I sauté Maui onions with the purslane in local butter until it turns a dark brown, adding garlic and turmeric, tamari, and bone broth made from local venison. Local mozzarella goat cheese is grated on top, along with any leftover bread, and it gets put into the oven to broil. Perfect for a rainy Haiku day. I also regularly add it to tatziki, and ferment it into pickled things. The ferment in the jar below is a delicious combination of purlsane, daikon radish, garlic, ginger, turmeric, and salt.

Purslane was added to this ferment, as well as raw in the salad.

SHEEP SORREL

(Rumex acetosella)

Typically found at higher elevations on Kaua'i, Maui, and the Big Island, this little plant is native to Eurasia. Learn to recognize sheep sorrel's look and sour taste, and it becomes part of your lifelong wild food knowledge. That knowledge could be handy if utilized when you travel to places far from the isles of *Hawai'i nei*. This little plant is found nearly world wide, and is related to the sorrel that is grown in gardens or found at fancy restaurants in soup.

Leaves grow from a loose basal rosette and are succulent, but not very thick. Their stems (petioles) are slightly grooved and they send out characteristically bright red flower stalks. The leaves are unique, reminding whoever named the plant of a sheep's head with flared ears. The young leaves don't usually have the little flared wings at the base, but older ones do and will help you identify it. Leaves can taste astringent from plants that have gone to seed. Try adding raw greens to a salad, in spring rolls, on a sandwich, or thrown into cooked soups. They are great added to sauces put over potatoes or squash.

Tender young sheep sorrel greens, perfect for harvesting.

Keep your eyes open for the red seed tops of sheep sorrel. Photo courtesy of Forest & Kim Starr

43

SOW THISTLE

(Sonchus oleraceus)

I am a great lover of blueberries, but when it comes to antioxidants they get all of the attention! Pualele, or sow thistle as it's known in English, rivals those little blue berries in known antioxidants (16). You have to find its leaves and items at the right stage of growth to be delicious, but do so and you'll be singing in the rain, because you've found a nutritional gem for free. This is a bitter plant, and although it will still be bitter when harvested young, it will be much more palatable. The entire plant is edible, but I most often seek out its leaves, which I chiffonade (see more on page 34)

Tender young leaves and flower buds of sow thistle, perfect for harvesting. Photo courtesy of John Kallas, Wild Food Adventures

If you find yourself with an abundance of the greens you might try blanching and freezing them, adding to fermented vegetables, or dehydrating. If dehydrating, it has been shown that you can save more than 90% of the antioxidants if you keep the humidity out, so make sure to put them into a jar with a tightly fitting lid as soon as they're dehydrated (17). They can also be added to lasagna, mixed with salt fish and stuffed inside a breadfruit that's going to be baked over a fire, or added to saimin. *Sonchus asper* can also be found on some of the islands, but *Sonchus oleraceus* dominates.

This plant is glyphosate-resistant, meaning it has now joined the list of superweeds that have evolved resistance to RoundUp and other glyphosate-containing herbicides. It can accumulate nitrogen, so be careful about harvesting from any area that there is intensive non-organic agriculture. When I harvest from clean areas that I know are free of herbicides and pesticides, and don't have chemical fertilizers applied, I also like to make bitters.

Bitters are a great addition to a cocktail, or can be taken alone before or after a heavy meal to strengthen and tonify the digestive system. Skip the modern-day versions with high fructose corn syrup and fake flavors, and make your own. Use the strongest alcohol you can find and pour it over chopped up sow thistle that has been stuffed into a jar (you can chop up the entire plant, roots included). Fill to the top with alcohol, cover with a lid, label, and let sit in a dark area for one month. In a separate jar I like to combine nutmeg, cardamom, dried starfruit, chilis, cloves, wild fennel seeds, ginger root, peppercorns, vanilla beans, cacao nibs, coffee beans, orange rind and raw honey. Cover with alcohol and let sit for one month, then strain both jars and combine them. Bitters add a depth of flavor to things like alcoholic drinks, fruit salads, and popsicles. Try adding a drop of bitters to your mojitos, bourbon drinks, or mixed with orange juice.

WILD BITTERS

SPANISH NEEDLES

(Bidens alba var. radiata & B. pilosa)

Whether you live in Kula or Wailuku, Kaua'i or Molokai, the tender young greens of Spanish needles can usually be found. Known as kineh in Hawaiian, both species can be found on all of our inhabited islands. Most people know this as the plant whose seeds get stuck to your clothes when going out for a hike, which is why it is also known as hitchhiker plant. Harvest any new growth that looks

tender and vibrant. This is one that I prefer to cook. Kineh packs a powerful nutritional cocktail of phytonutrients (18). This plant grows year-round, so once you learn to harvest these tender greens you'll have an abundant supply.

Spanish needles growing out of weed mat.

Spanish needle seeds. Photo Courtesy Forest & Kim Starr

47

WILD AMARANTH

(Amaranthus dubius, A. hybridus, A. spinosus, A. viridis)

Tender young wild amaranth greens.

People working in the cane fields, or other monocropped agriculture on the islands, usually laugh at the notion of eating wild amaranth. Spiny amaranth (*Amaranthus spinosus*) in particular, with its sharp spines, gets a good chuckle because it's a major agricultural pest. All of the wild amaranth species are packed with vitamins, minerals, and phytonutrients, along with some protein.

Tender young sprouts of *Amaranthus dubius* are an excellent source of protein, containing all of the essential amino acids except for leucine (19). *Amaranthus hybridus* has been shown to have appreciable amounts of macronutrients (fat, protein, carbohydrate), micronutrients (vitamins and minerals) and phytochemicals like hydrocyanic acid (20). *Amaranthus spinosus* is an excellent source of iron and calcium (21). I always cook these wild greens, use like spinach, and will use the cooking water in sauces or to cook other vegetables if it tastes good.

Tender young spiny amaranth in the perfect stage for harvesting and eating, just be sure to avoid any and all spines. Photo courtesy of Forest & Kim Starr

Did you miss the tender young greens stage? No worries, mature leaves of the plants can also be harvested and cooked. Seeds provide yet another food source, and although it's a lot of work, can be more easily separated by cutting the plant stalks and drying them. Once dried, thrash them on tarps and winnow out any debris. I also became familiar with using ashes of plants while living on the Navajo Reservation in Arizona. Juniper, cedar and tumbleweed ash were added in small amounts during the cooking of corn, beans, and bread on the rez. We have all of those plants on Maui, but the ashes of amaranth can also be used.

Wild Amaranth is here to stay, so befriend it and you will have a delicious and nutritious ally your whole life long. This plant has an incredibly long history of use, with various species utilized by ancient cultures around the globe. Spiny amaranth is officially a superweed, having become resistant to glyphosate. As the main active ingredient in RoundUp, glyphosate has been severely overused around the planet. It begs the question: when will we work harmoniously with our environment and stop blasting the earth with an onslaught of chemical inputs?

A RICH VENISON BONE BROTH, *made with turmeric, ginger, garlic, lemongrass, keffir lime, miso, tamari, sesame oil, sesame seeds, and chives does well with the addition of wild amaranth greens.*

Feral

FRUITS

Have you heard of Fallen Fruit? Yes, of course that stuff rotting on the ground because no one was hungry enough to pick it up, but what I'm talking about is a group who creates maps guiding you to fruit trees found in urban areas around the globe. They also hold Fruit Jams where people get together and make jam, and have art projects inspired by the abundance of fruit that went from unwanted to loved. They are inspirational, and I dream of one day having mapping programs and apps available here on the islands to assist us in the charge of never letting another piece of fruit fall to the ground. When it rains it pours in regards to fruit, and what better opportunity do we have to gather with our community of friends to create memories and nourishment.

The following pages are just a teaser when considering the smorgasboard of fruits available on the islands. Loquats (*Eriobotrya japonica*) rain down at higher elevations and can be found naturalized, feral papaya (*Carica papaya*) is never far at lower elevations, along with noni (*Morinda citrifolia*), feral coffee cherries (*Fragaria vesca*), and abandoned mountain apples (*Syzygium malaccense*), known as ohi'a 'ai in Hawaiian. We have bitter gourd (*Momordica charantia*), where ONLY the bright red fleshy mass surrounding the seed, called the aril, is eaten and the seeds are spit out. *Monstera deliciosa*'s phallic fruit is eaten once it has fully ripened, and elderberries (*Sambucus mexicana*) can be eaten once cooked or dehydrated. The snake-like fruits of trumpet tree (*Cecropia obtusifolia*) can be eaten. Although the following can be found in the wild, our native ecosystems are in desperate need of our help, so try planting endemic 'ohelo berries

'Ohelo berries kissed by morning dew. Photo Courtesy of Forest & Kim Starr

(*Vaccinium reticulatum*), ohia' ha (*Syzygium sandwicense*), and *Diospyros sandwicensis*, assuring that future generations will be able to enjoy them. The Hawaii Tropical Fruit Growers provide a wealth of experienced people who can guide you in your quest for fruit.

BANANA

(Musa spp.)

Do you remember your first banana harvest? It is nearly a rite of passage for those of us living in the jungle, and I oftentimes take new farm volunteers who come to stay with us out for that first experience. This is one plant, technically an herb, which could be feeding our islands in much greater quantity. For a forager willing to swing a machete and carry the heavy haul, it is well worth the effort.

Bananas are known as mai'a in Hawaiian. Most people don't know that green unripe bananas can be eaten, and it is mostly for that reason that I include them here. In my house a knife is dedicated to removing the peels, which contains a sticky sap, and they are then put in a pot to boil. They can be fried, blended, grated into hashbrowns, or put into soups. The flowers are also edible, and the non-edible leaves are utilized so frequently as plates and wraps in my kitchen as to make them an indispensable part of my life.

My son Saelyn's first word was banana, and many a child has started their entry into solid foods with this fruit. But do not forget the value of utilizing green bananas for weaning babies, whose carotenoids (precursors to vitamin A) are made more bioavailable when the bananas are boiled and eaten with amaranth greens (22, 23). Wild greens and green bananas are a fabulous way to grow healthy kids, and it was this combination that was my son Zeb's first solids. Ditch the instant cereal for real food!

Rack of wild bananas with large flower. Wait until green bananas are fully grown before harvesting.

GUAVA

(Psidium guajava, P. cattleianum, P. cattleianum var. lucidum Hort.)

Guava is a favorite in our household. The flavor sends me over the moon, and is quite different depending on if it is raw or cooked. My son harvests them liberally, while on his way to school or out playing in the neighborhood with friends, making for one happy mom. In my kitchen they find their way into sweet things like raw pies, malasadas, and guava sorbet. But they also go well with fish, poultry, wild boar, and venison.

Common Guava

You might have seen it on a car in front of you or in the parking lot; that bumper sticker *Guava Happens* has provided a few good chuckles. Life is full of unpredictable events,

Ripe common guava

which is why we can all resonate with the term *sh*t happens*. And guava does happen, as many a person can attest to when they step on a rotting guava and it squishes up between the toes. But if anything is predictable, it is that we will continue to have guava. This little tree is a super producer, with multiple harvests a year. Foragers in the tropics or sub-tropics can keep their larders full year-round with delicacies made from this plant alone. Although not many people eat it straight off the tree, you'll find few who dislike

it once processed. Guava is chockablock full of nutrients, and blasts ahead of nearly all other fruits in vitamin C. We heard about lycopene in tomatoes, and then it was watermelon. Now we find out there's more lycopene in guava than either of those two (24). I can only imagine what the nutritional content is in my POG, that's passionfruit, orange, and guava juice for those of you who don't live in Hawai'i.

WILD POG: *passionfruit, orange, and guava juice.*

Common guava flower.

Immature guava fruits. Try pickling them before they turn yellow

Guava is a climacteric fruit, so it will continue ripening after it has been harvested. This means that you can harvest fruits that are full size, but still firm and slightly green. This is great, as ripe guavas can literally turn to mush by the time you get home. Guava goes from underripe to overripe in short order, so I harvest large quantities that are still firm and process them over the next two to three days as they ripen. I make fresh juice by cutting ripe guava in half and scooping out the center, but you can also leave the skins on if you like. This goes into the blender with enough water to cover. After a few pulses of the blender I put this slurry into a nut milk bag or strainer to remove the seeds. This is a thick juice, of course more water can be added, and it is excellent drunk immediately or used in things like raw pies.

It can also be frozen, or used in fruit leathers.

I most often turn to using a cooked method to get my juice though, as I can process a lot more guava this way. Guava are washed, cut in half, and placed into a pot. Just enough water to cover is added. The pot is slowly brought to a boil, and then removed from the heat so that the guava can cool. Once cool enough to touch, I scoop them into my nut milk bag and let it hang over a bowl. Squeeze the bag to get the thicker and more pulpy parts to come through and compost the rest. There are two products that it actually makes, a clear juice and a thick pulp that settles to the bottom. Both can have totally different applications in the kitchen, but whatever I don't use right away gets put back into the pot, slowly brought to a boil, and immediately put into sterilized canning jars and sealed with new lids. No sugar is added.

Halved guavas in just enough water to cover.

FERAL GUAVA SAUCE

6 cups guava juice

6 cups quartered ohi'a 'ai

3 cups honey

2 crushed cloves

8 wild cinnamon leaves

8 wild allspice leaves

Hawaiian sea salt to taste

Combine all ingredients.

Bring to a boil, then turn down the heat and simmer for 15 minutes.

Remove wild cinnamon and wild allspice leaves.

Mix in blender, then return to pot and cook to desired consistency.

Cooked guava straining through a nut milk bag.

CANNED GUAVA JUICE WITH PULP
SETTLED TO THE BOTTOM.

VENISON WITH FERAL GUAVA SAUCE, *mustard, wild greens,*

and poi. Feral guava sauce is quite versatile and can be made into a delicious barbeque sauce when cooking meat. Use it to glaze pheasant, wild boar ribs, or served with venison. Maui's venison distributor is Royal Hawaiian Venison at www.mauideer.info.

You can usually find a jar of poached guava shells in my fridge. We regularly eat them with cheese, a pairing of flavors that is popular throughout the Caribbean and South America. This recipe makes for roughly 2 quart jars, and after you have used up the shells the delicious syrup can be mixed with fizzy water for a natural soda, made into popsicles, served over ice cream, or drunk straight from the jar.

POACHED GUAVA SHELLS IN SYRUP

2 ¼ cups kiawe syrup, see page 113

4 ½ cups strong wild allspice tea

2 cups organic cane sugar

Combine all ingredients in a shallow pot. Cook on medium heat until sugar is dissolved. Add guava halves, making sure not to add too many, and gently spoon the syrup over them as they cook for roughly 2-3 minutes. Put one wild allspice leaf into each jar and gently transfer shells into sterilized jars. Cover with syrup and seal tightly with a lid. Cool and then refrigerate.

STUFFED GUAVA SHELL *with homemade fromagina cheese, feral fennel seeds,*
popolo berries, strawberry and mint.

HALVED GUAVA SHELLS, *ready to be poached on rear burner. Center pulp and seeds are removed and made into fresh juice.*

STRAWBERRY GUAVA

Waiawi, as it's known in Hawaiian, comes in red or yellow varieties. This is one of my all-time favorites, and its rich and complex flavor speaks to its amazing nutritional power (25). Although the little yellow waiawi provide more health-promoting qualities than

many things you find at the grocery store, it is red waiawi that maintains its position at the top, with nearly double the amount of phenolic compounds and higher levels of vitamin C (26).

Introduced in 1825 as an ornamental, strawberry guava has become one of the most invasive plants we know in the Hawaiian Islands. They are reducing the amount of water captured in our mauka forests and crowding out our sacred natives. Large areas of rotting fruit proliferates swarms of fruit flies that also invade agricultural lands. Guava is an anomaly, providing foragers and nutritionists with a pinnacle dream food, while at the same time a nightmare for conservationists as it radically changes Hawaii's landscape.

Strawberry guava forest, with not much else growing.

Eat guava fresh out of hand, spitting out its hard seeds, or strain out its fruit pulp to use in sweet or savory dishes. Try your hand at making a wine. Its wood has been used to smoke sea salt and meat, and its leaves used for tea. It's easy to get turned around in a strawberry guava forest, so tune into the direction of the sun and the sound of running water to help guide you home.

STRAWBERRY GUAVA'S JUICE *will store in the refrigerator for only a day or two before fermenting. All canned juice should be used within 4 months, and stored in a cool dark place, to retain as much of its health promoting qualities as possible (27).*

JAVA PLUMS

(Syzygium cumini)

This little elliptical fruit ripens to a dark purple black. Listen for the chorus of myna birds, clueing you into a tree full of ripe fruits. The birds and the tree are native to India, where it is said Lord Rama lived on the fruits while being exiled to the forest for 14 years.

Java plum bears many fruits. Photo Courtesy of The 3 Foragers

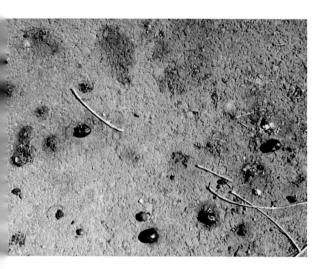

Java plums stain the ground, a common scene in Hawaii.

If you are going to eat java plums raw, it is best to try fruits before harvesting, as they come in a range of flavors. I like to poke them with a fork, sprinkle with salt, and cool in the refrigerator before eating raw. After the seed has been removed its pulp can be added to smoothies, fruit leather, galettes, or made into a beautiful syrup. But it is in savory dishes where this fruit really shines. It makes fabulous chutney when mixed with ingredients like Maui onion, ginger, feral fennel seeds, Hawaiian chilis and Molokai black salt. Try adding it to your teriyaki sauce, or making barbeque sauce or wine. It is yet another nutritional superstar (are you starting to see a pattern here?), loaded with antioxidants that outperform its close relative jaboticaba (28, 29).

Large biotech companies use Hawai'i as a testing ground for pesticides and GMO's. Afraid you've been exposed to pesticides? Making sure our bodies are nourished well is our first line of defense, but Java plums were recently researched and shown to have protective effects against pesticide-induced cardiotoxicity (30).

NATAL PLUMS

(Carissa macrocarpa)

This is not really a wild plant, but it is so widely planted and produces so much fruit, that I decided to highlight it here anyway. Hardly anyone knows that these fruits are edible once they turn bright red, and they are a gift that keeps on giving with multiple harvests per year. They grow in parking lots all over Kahului on Maui, so are a frequent snack on trips to town. Plantings started somewhere around 1905 on the islands, where this shrub was brought from South Africa. It also produces beautiful white flowers that are star-shaped. Those flowers are often confused with jasmine, and smell so divine that I use them in herbal baths, infused oils, and aromatic powders.

You can eat the entire immune-boosting fruit, including its skin and small seeds (31). Be prepared for the white sap that leaks out of them, and double thorns. Warnings are regularly given about not cooking this fruit in aluminum due to an interaction with the sap, and the sap can make for a mess to clean up when cooking (use oil to remove). But the sap is of no harm to you, and it is this little fruit that brings us the closest here in the subtropics to a cranberry flavor. Try making a natal plum, orange rind, and pineapple relish at your Thanksgiving meal. Or a marinated kale salad with chopped fresh natal plum and Big Island goat feta cheese. num num!

This natal plum hedge near my home extends for several hundred feet.

PASSIONFRUIT

(Passiflora edulis, P. tarminiana)

Passiflora edulis flower.

Passiflora edulis and Passiflora laurifolia fruits.

If I had a daughter, Lilikoi would be her name. People have been passionate about passionfruit for a very long time, with its exotic flowers and juicy fruits that just beg for romantic poetry. We have over a dozen *Passiflora* species on Maui alone, and although I haven't tried all of them, the following are reported to be edible: *P. edulis, P. foetida, P. incarnata, P. laurifolia, P. ligularis, P. manicata, P. quadrangularis, P. tarminiana, P. vitifolia.* Vines can become quite aggressive, and banana poka (*P. tarminiana*) is a serious invasive in the PoliPoli Spring State Recreation Area on Maui. It's the fruits of *P. edulis* that I find wild most often, and its juice regularly becomes tea or is frozen in ice cube trays to have on hand for later.

Paula Fuga is one of my all-time favorite musical artists, and her first album is a testament to her love for lilikoi.
Image Courtesy of Paula Fuga

Image on left: Banana poka engulfing power lines. Photo courtesy of Forest & Kim Starr

Image below: Banana poka flower

Banana poka fruits in varying stages of ripeness.

When eating banana poka do not spit seeds on the ground, as they will germinate. Photo Courtesy of Forest & Kim Starr

THE PULP AND SEEDS OF LILIKOI (P. EDULIS) *and*

Jamaican lilikoi (P. laurifolia) are scooped out and put into a blender. That slurry is combined with other fruits like banana, jackfruit, or guava, and the mixture is spread as thinly as possible on teflex sheets or parchment paper and dehydrated into fruit leather.

POHA BERRIES

(Physalis peruviana)

Poha berry flower.

These little fruits are so much fun. When you find them it's as if you've been on a magical treasure hunt and the prize has been lovingly wrapped in beautiful packaging. The fruits resemble lanterns hanging from the stems in their sheaths, and hold a golden light within. They should not be harvested until they reach that golden yellow color, as their flavor and nutrition improve when allowed to fully ripen (32). They are reported on all of our inhabited islands, except Ni'ihau, having naturalized themselves here from the Andes Mountains of Peru and Ecuador.

I rarely make it home with any of these, as they are best eaten fresh out of hand (discard the papery sheaths). But if you do find yourself with an abundance at your fingertips, they are fabulous in fresh salsa, chutney, jam, or dehydrated into a chewy raisin-like treat. The best cake I have ever made was a custardy poha berry bundt cake, served at our Christmas meal in 2012.

Poha berries held in their papery sheaths.

These fruits are a gift, little packages with a range of antioxidants that work synergistically with the body to get rid of the oxidative damage that leads to disease and aging (33, 34). They are said to have some liver protecting qualities and add delightfully delicious diversity to the diet (35).

POPOLO BERRIES

(Solanum americanum)

These plants are widespread, being found on all of
our inhabited islands. Their little berries are edible
and taste somewhat like tomatoes, but they have a
unique flavor that is all their own. ONLY eat the
fully ripened shiny dark purple/black berries, with
no tinge of green left on them. They make for a
nice trailside nibble, and are an ingredient in an
incredible steak sauce made by Mia and Pascal at
Transitional Gastronomy.

*Popolo berry plants are welcomed in my gardens,
and bear many fruits over a long period of time.*

*Perfectly ripe popolo berries. Shiny
purple/black berries should have no
traces of green.*

A BREAKFAST FULL OF PURPLE POWER.

Popolo berries are a fun garnish, but are also great cooked in pan-fried purple sweet potatoes with Maui onion, garlic, and cooked water hyacinth flowers. Served with a fried egg, purple Jamaican vervain flowers, and the wild spice mix found on page 108.

PANINI

(Opuntia ficus-indica)

Panini habitat

Bust out your gloves, tongs, and buckets. You will need to channel some of that paniolo toughness to harvest these. To me it's worth it to cowgirl up and wrangle some of these delicious fruits, both for their unique taste, which is reminiscent of melon, and for the outstanding nutrition found in the pads and flowers (133, 134). This plant is also known as prickly pear. Great care is needed to protect yourself from the spines and tiny glochids when harvesting and processing. Do not touch them with your bare hands! To remove the spines and glochids on the fruits or pads, singe them over an open flame, rub in some sand, and rinse thoroughly with water. This is where you entice friends to help you with the lure of panini margaritas, teriyaki flavored prickly pear pad jerky, or some kiawe waffles with panini syrup.

We have whitish-green and pink varieties here on Maui, as well as *Opuntia cochenillifera*. Young pads are fantastic barbequed on the grill and served sliced with eggs. Nopales, as they're known in Spanish, have long been used in the treatment of diabetes, and research continues to justify this claim (36). One panini, two panini, three panini, four…makes me want to eat a whole lot more!

Panini fruits can be found in yellow, and this magenta pink. Photo Courtesy of Forest & Kim Starr

RUBUS SPP.

(Rubus niveus, R. rosifolius, R. hawaiensis)

Berry picking holds a special place in most people's hearts. Even those who find this wild food thing highly unrealistic and a waste of time, will delight upon a perfectly ripened berry. Maybe it's because our bodies innately know the incredible health-promoting effects they hold (37). Berries are part of the Rose Family, and their thorny brambles protect something quite divine.

We have many *Rubus* species on the islands, and many of them are finicky in flavor. *Rubus argutus, R. discolor, R. ellipticus, R. glaucus*, and *R. sieboldii* can all be found. Even if some of them have berries that aren't quite to your liking, the creative chef doesn't let something so beautiful in color and so nourishing to the body just slip by unloved. They can be added to smoothies, butter, mixed with other fruits into jam, or put into a sauce. Besides the hill raspberries, vinegar is where I mostly turn to with the *Rubus spp.*, as it does an excellent job of extracting all the goodness. Berry vinegars are something beautiful to behold.

Hill Raspberry

Hill Raspberry, form b, ripe and ready to harvest

Hill raspberry (*R. niveus*) goes by many names, but it is mostly known as 'the delicious one'. My son Saelyn begs to go and harvest these berries, bringing a smile to mom's face. We will sit and fantasize about them for hours, filled with anticipation of another seasons harvest. They can be eaten with wild abandon, as this plant has officially made the noxious weed list (38). Naturalized on Maui, Kaua'i, and Hawai'i, there is a 'form b' that is specific to Maui's Kula and Poli Poli areas.

Thimbleberry

Found at lower elevations in our wet jungles, thimbleberry (*Rubus rosifolius*) can vary in flavor. I have found some that were sweet and delicious, and some that were quite bland. Regardless, they are always a welcome site to me and make for a delightful trail nibble. Like all the other *Rubus spp.* berries, it has powerful phytonutrients (39). This plant became an ally for me while pregnant with my son Zeb. I have no idea of any scientific evidence of its effectiveness as compared to the well-researched and popular red raspberry leaf (*R. idaeus*), but I used its leaves regularly for tea. Flower petals are also edible.

Thimbleberry

WILD BERRY COCKTAIL . *Depending on the sweetness of the Rubus spp. you've harvested, berries do well infused into alcohol like vodka. Add sugar to make a cordial, or try making a wild berry shrub.*

Âkala

This plant is a living link with ancient Hawai'i. And I mean so ancient that it was here long before anyone inhabited these islands and spoke their name. `Akala (*Rubus hawaiensis*) is one of our endemic species, so it is found nowhere else on earth. Being that we have already lost a huge number of our endemic species in the great tragedy of biodiversity loss, it is with the utmost respect and warning of caution that I include it here. This is a sacred plant. I feel that if we do not learn to love it, then we have no grounded basis from which to dream it into our future. For me 'akala is a to be eaten on special occasions, with an awareness of what it truly is. Whenever I harvest `akala, or our endemic 'ōhelo *(Vaccinium reticulatum)* berries, I speak with them candidly about our beautiful existence and thank them for the blessing I am about to receive.

`Akala, which means pink in Hawaiian, are the largest berries I have ever harvested. According to the Smithsonian's Hawaii Flora plant website, they can be found on the islands of Kaua'i, Moloka'i, Maui, and Hawai'i. I have a difficult time making it home with hill raspberries, as I can hardly contain myself from eating them all, but `akala is different. The flavor is both astringent and bitter. I can't help but think of Pele while harvesting these high on the mountain, with her sometimes hard to swallow powerful, passionate, and volcanic nature. I was stumped for awhile on what to do with these giant berries, but received some inspiration when remembering 'akala is a member of the Rose Family. The berries go through some kitchen magic when mixed with homegrown aromatic rose petals (*Rosa spp.*) and feral red clover blossoms (*Trifolium pratense var. sativum*) in live apple cider vinegar.

'Akala with ripe berries

Pele vinegar is a beautiful red.

SEA GRAPES

(Coccoloba uvifera)

Unripe sea grapes.

These fruits are so venusian to me. I can almost see Dionysus plucking them from their long druping racemes as a gift for Aphrodite. They are absolutely beautiful, and exude a gentle strength with their thick leaves and flexible branches. Native to tropical and sub-tropical parts of the Americas, they are not related to grapes. As part of the buckwheat family, they are more closely botanically related to our wild leafy green sheep sorrel (*Rumex acetosella*). This way of observing plant families, by noticing their structures and patterns, opens us up to a whole new way of seeing our brothers and sisters in the plant nation.

Sea grape trees thrive on salty shorelines, holding up stoically to a battery of salt and wind. They were the most common tree, along with beach almond (*Terminalia catappa*), that I saw hugging the shorelines as we sailed through the Caribbean Islands, northern South America, and Central America. Unlike Hawai'i, where they regularly fruit, I was hard pressed to find them bearing in abundance. I did, however, learn to take advantage of a replenishable source of disposable plates. Their large leathery round leaves can quickly be gathered, wiped down, and used to put pupu's or solid things like quiche on. And what about the fruits? The ones I've eaten have always been delicious, although I do hear some people say there are bland ones out there. They have a large seed, which is not eaten. Spitting out the seeds while sitting at the beach reminds me of times spent snacking on sunflower seeds with my Grandpa. This snacking ritual of seed spitting is revitalized with a new generation, but with a different food. They ripen irregularly, so once they have begun to turn a pinkish/purplish color I like to cut them and bring them home for a vase. Just pluck them off as they ripen, and you can even use the leaves as plates.

Sea grapes ripening in a vase at home.

The Aloha Spirit is alive and well in our *Hawai'i nei*, and flowers are a physical manifestation of that love incarnate. Flowers adorn our hair, with women signaling men in the dance of courtship by wearing a flower tucked behind their right ear if 'available' and behind the left if 'unavailable'. We find them on our cell phone covers, bumper stickers, beach towels, and our infamous aloha shirts and muumuus. Of course not all lei are made from flowers, but the vast majority are, and nearly every special event or ceremony has us wrapping each other, or the land, with lei. Anniversaries, weddings, graduations, birthdays, funerals, and airport arrivals still see this ritual in action. Usually their beauty is fleeting, so we celebrate and enjoy a few shared moments of pleasure. The flowers will die, but the memories will not.

Eating wild flowers is my sacrament. Jokes are made that I'm part of the flower eating tribe. With such a large number of wild and underutilized flowers in Hawai'i, it's a fine spot for me to be. This chapter covers nine wild edible flowers found on the islands, but also keep your eyes out for *Rubus spp.* flower petals, red clover (*Trifolium pratense var. sativum*), sweet white clover *(Melilotus albus)*, panini blossoms, begonia, male papaya flowers, wild black mustard flowers, false awa inflourescence (*Piper auritum)*, mallow, milo (*Thespesia populnea*), banana, *Oxalis spp.,* and Spanish needles. Some are used as garnish, frozen into ice cubes, or whipped into butter. Others

Feral night-blooming cereus flower (Hylocereus undatus).

are cooked, soaked in cream, or soaked in lime juice. Some even hold their color when blended with sugar to create beautifully colored sweets. Adventurous experimenters are encouraged to dabble with the abundant night-blooming cereus (*Hylocereus undatus*), as unopened flower buds and flowers can be eaten cooked. Large stands have gone feral, and without their native pollinators on the islands those flowers cannot become dragonfruit. But they can become dinner…so much to discover! May you be blessed with wild food knowledge that blossoms into a beautiful flower.

ELDERFLOWER

(Sambucus mexicana)

Used around the world for food, medicine, and utility, elder has enchanted a great many of us throughout the halls of time. It is included in the myths and old folklore of many in our human family, and has now naturalized on the islands of Kaua'i, Oahu, Maui, and the Big Island. Look for its compound leaves and large white flower umbels, which turn into dark purple berries. I have found it growing in wet jungle, to nearly 4,000 ft. elevation, so it has adapted easily to a variety of growing conditions.

The flowers can be made into syrup, tea, frozen in ice cubes, infused into vinegar, or added to the batters of things like pancakes or muffins. My friend Wendy Petty at *Hunger and Thirst* has a recipe for elderflower buttermilk sherbet I would highly recommend trying. So, should you find yourself skipping along and notice a sprinkling of tiny white flowers on the ground, look up to see if you are standing under a graceful elder.

Elderflowers grow in umbels.

Elderflower habitat

Elderflower tempura and elderflower champagne are how these flowers most often find their way into my diet. There's such a feeling of merriment when I think of this plant, and of the justified and much-needed pleasure they provide. Many a party has been had, with friends and family, sipping elderflower champagne as the elderflower fritters fry. Tempura is easy to make by mixing one egg, one cup of flour, and one cup of cold water. Flowers, still attached to their umbel, are dipped in the chilled mixture and then put into hot coconut oil. To top it off, my auntie in Kula grows lavender, and I like to infuse it into sugar, powder that infused sugar, and then sprinkle it over the hot elderblow as they come out of the pan.

Elderblow, as the flowers are also called, have natural yeast that is nearly fail-safe when fermenting. My great-aunt, god bless her feisty flamboyant soul, would have had no qualms telling you that this is no champagne as it is not made with champagne grapes. She was the Countess d'Eudeville from the Champagne region of France after all! The recipe on the following page comes from my foraging friend Leda Meredith, a master wild food preserver and author.

ELDERFLOWER CHAMPAGNE

Makes 4 Quarts

INGREDIENTS

7 to 8 large (6 inch or so diameter) or double that of smaller elderflower clusters

2 pints boiling rainwater, or filtered water

6 pints cold rainwater, or filtered water

1 pound honey OR 1 1/2 pounds sugar

1/4 cup cider vinegar OR 2 large lemons (juice & rind) plus 2 tablespoons cider vinegar

PREPARATION

1. Do not wash the flowers. Remove thick stalks and any debris.

2. Place the honey or sugar in a very large bowl and pour in the 2 pints of boiling water. Stir until the honey or sugar has completely dissolved.

3. Add the 6 pints of cold water. Stir in the vinegar or lemon juice and the elderflowers.

4. Cover with a clean dishtowel and let the mixture sit at room temperature for 48 hours, stirring at least twice a day. By the end of these two days you should see signs of fermentation: the top of the liquid will look frothy and bubbly, especially when you stir it.

5. Pour the fermenting elderflower champagne through a finely meshed sieve to strain out the flowers (and lemon rind, if using). Use a funnel to help transfer the brew into clean plastic soda-type bottles with screw tops or thick ceramic or beer bottles with flip tops. Do not use corked wine bottles because elderflower champagne is quite capable of popping out the corks or worse, exploding the bottles. Leave at least an inch of headspace between the surface of the liquid and the rims of the bottles. Secure the tops.

6. Leave at room temperature for a week, "burping" (opening briefly) the bottles at least once a day. After the week at room temperature, move them to the refrigerator, but keep "burping" the bottles occasionally for another week.

Elderflower champagne will keep in the refrigerator for several months. The honey version takes slightly longer to ferment out than the sugar version .

elderflower
(Sambucus mexicana)
6/21/2014

Dried elderflowers

HIBISCUS

(Hibiscus tiliaceus, H. rosa-sinensis, Malvaviscus penduliflorus)

I often marvel at hau (*Hibiscus tiliaceus*), first for making such a long journey packed in the hulls of early Polynesian sailing canoes, and secondly for their phenomenal power of transformation. As the day begins, a vibrant yellow flower opens to greet the new day. By the afternoon its petals have transformed to a light orange. And by evening, they have turned a burnt orangey-red and die. How I say? Why? Their mystery is yet to be unlocked, but I welcome the mystery into me when I eat it. This plant forms hugely dense thickets, and is wonderful for feeding large groups of people with its plentiful flowers. I typically tempura the petals, which contain antioxidants (40), but they can also be eaten raw or sautéed.

Red hibiscus (*Hibiscus rosa-sinensis*) and Turk's Cap (*Malvaviscus penduliflorus*) are also regulars. It is the Turk's Cap that most often go feral on the windward sides.

Young hau flower. Hau can be eaten raw, sautéed, or tempura

Red hibiscus flowers are both beautiful and edible.

95

RICE PAPER ROLLS
with red hibiscus and Jamaican vervain flowers.

JAMAICAN VERVAIN

(Stachytarpheta cayennensis, Stachytarpheta jamaicensis)

This is probably my most used wild edible flower, simply because it grows in quantity right out my own front door. And the back door, and the side door! These common little flowers provide the forager with an abundant supply of nectar-filled cups, and most people agree they taste like mushrooms.

The two Stachytarpheta referenced look nearly identical and can be difficult to tell apart. They can hybridize as well, so I get botanically lazy and call them both Jamaican vervain. They are also known as blue porterweed and belong to the Verbena Family (Verbenaceae). They're a great place to view bees and butterflies, who can easily be seen working the flower inflorescences for their nectar. Pictured on the right is my Aunt Dorothy's preserved kumquats with vanilla bean seeds, yogurt, begonia flower, and Jamaican vervain flowers. The mushroom taste is very faint, so don't let it stop you from adding such beauty to your sweet treats as well.

Jamaican vervain flowers.

NASTURTIUM

(Tropaeolum majus)

Large stands of nasturtium can be found at upper elevations on Maui, and are reportedly found on Kaua'i, Molokai, and the Big Island. The flavor of these flowers is spicy and warming, oftentimes compared with the taste of papaya seeds. They are beautiful in salads, but also pair wonderfully with meats. Add them to a venison sandwich, or stew, or put them into miso. They pack a powerful nutritional punch and continue to be researched for their beneficial qualities (41, 42, 43).

Nasturtium gone feral.

Flowers are typically red, orange, or yellow.

WILD GINGER

(Hedychium coronarium, H. flavescens)

Many of the ginger plants that have
naturalized on the islands have edible flowers,
but the flowers of white butterfly ginger
and yellow butterfly ginger are what I have
most experience with. They can be found
on nearly all of our islands, and I have seen
them growing from the coast up to 4,000 ft.
in elevation. Both the opened and unopened
flowers can be eaten. I like to remove the
stamens on opened flowers prior to eating raw
because they are a bit rough, after which they
make nice raw additions to salads and spring
rolls. They are delicious when sautéed in butter
with Maui onions until browned. They can
be soaked in cream and baked into custardy
things, or dried and put into herbal teas.

*Yellow butterfly ginger flowers. Photo
Courtesy of Forest & Kim Starr*

I like to add the flowers to herbal baths, or
steam distill them into hydrosol. They make
for lovely edible bouquets. Cut the stems,
with flowers, and put into a vase with plenty
of water. Use the flowers and buds at your
convenience. The flowers are made into
lei, and if you find a Cuban around, their
eyes might light up if you gift them a white
butterfly ginger lei, as that is their country's
national flower.

*Butterfly ginger flowers are delicious with
cream and eggs. This quiche, with a kiawe
crust, was cooked in a solar oven.*

Nuts, beans, and seeds are charged with carrying on their species. Those potentials of regeneration are encoded with instructions on how to grow, along with the nutrients they need to get started. Should you find yourself lucky enough to stumble upon these packages of potential, and should they be from a plant deemed safe for human consumption, rejoice in knowing you have been gifted a gem. Nutritionally, they compliment the wild greens, feral fruits, and wild edible flowers, because although those plants are strong performers in vitamins, minerals, and carbohydrates, they oftentimes don't contain much protein.

Purslane seeds, wild amaranth seeds, feral coffee (*Coffea arabica*) and papaya seeds are all appreciated as food at my house. I regularly get sustenance from the wild grasses of the *Poaceae* Family. Once making sure there is no mold growing on them, wild grass seeds can be harvested in quantity. I typically toast them in a cast iron skillet, removing any stems or chaff, and they are put into my mortar and pestle and ground up with salt and spices. This mixture is used to season foods and add nutrients.

Job's tears could be a potential food source, if we could figure out how to effectively remove their shells.

BEACH ALMOND

(Terminalia catappa)

Learn this one here in Hawai'i and you're set with some useful knowledge while traveling near tropical and sub-tropical shorelines around the world. This was definitely the most common tree I saw lining the shores of the Caribbean, with sea grapes (*Coccoloba uvifera*) coming in a close second. The nutmeat of beach almonds are admittedly difficult to get to, but they are an absolute delight once you do. The husk has a fibrousy flesh, that although is technically edible, I've never found very interesting to eat. Get through all that spongy, corky material, and inside is held a nutmeat about the size of a slivered almond. They are delicious, and a great source of protein, carbohydrate and fiber (44).

If I were ruler of the world I would put more money into research and development of a machine that could crack open these nuts effectively. As it stands now, they are mostly eaten as a nibble at the beach where they can be smashed open with a rock and the nutmeat picked out. They are also in my ceremony or special occasion food category due to all the love poured into processing them. The leaf of this tree most often makes it into my kitchen as disposable plates. Wiped clean, the leaves can be used to hold non-liquid foods. I've been to many a beach barbeque with plastic and paper plates blowing down the beach, which kind of breaks my heart when I see them end up in our ocean. So, now you've got an eco-friendly version whether you forgot your plates or are just one of those earth-loving types.

Beach almond has edible nuts, and its leaves work well as plates.

BEACH ALMONDS LOOK DIFFERENTLY AS THEY AGE.

The nutmeat is found in the center, and can be seen peeking out from the cracked open husk at the bottom of the page.

Photo Courtesy of The 3 Foragers

FERAL GUAVA SYRUP IS THE BASE OF THESE DELICIOUS BEACH ALMOND CANDIES,

which combines toasted beach almonds, grated dehydrated coconut, and guava. Cooking sugar to varying temperatures creates different textures of candy. Use this chart as a rough guide, as all these candymaking stages are truly made delicious with the addition of beach almonds. These candies were cooked to the firm ball stage, with almonds and coconut stirred in at the end. Once the candy has cooled and is safe to handle, it can be rolled in parchment paper and stored in an airtight container or in the refrigerator.

Stage	Temperature
Thread	223-234°F
Soft Ball	234-241°F
Firm Ball	242-248°F
Hard Ball	249-266°F
Soft Crack	270-290°F
Hard Crack	296-310°F
Caramel	320-350°F

COCONUT

(Cocos nucifera)

Sprouted coconut has a unique taste and foamy texture.

Oh the wonderful things we can do with coconut! I am definitely loco for cocos. Known as niu in Hawaiian, this has got to be the most utilized palm tree on the planet. Coconut water, coconut milk, and coconut oil now sit on grocery store shelves across America. But there are a few lesser known ways to bring this amazing plant into your kitchen, like sautéing the meat when it is just between jelly and firm meat, or putting it raw in salads. As a forager you are most likely to find coconuts that have already fallen to the ground and sprouted. Eating the foamy interior of sprouted coconut raw, flash fried, or put into sauces is a wild food widely available to the forager. If ever landscapers or natural disaster brings down a coconut palm, do not let the heart go to waste. The heart can be cut out near the top of the tree and provides pounds and pounds (did I mention pounds and pounds!) of delicious food.

MAKING COCONUT FLOUR

I sheepishly admit that there were years where I made coconut milk and threw out the remaining pulp. Little did I know this material could be made into what would become a staple ingredient in my kitchen. Flour made from dehydrating and grinding that leftover pulp can be used in baked goods, sauces, added to smoothies, etc. I've also found that if you don't spread the flour so thinly in the dehydrator, but instead form it into little clumps, and then only partially dehydrate it, you can create chewy pieces of coconut that smell of baked bread but have a meaty texture. You can add spices to these before dehydrating, or try marinating and serving them as pupus. We are limited only by our culinary imaginations when dealing with the versatile coconut.

1. *Put firm coconut meat into blender.*

2. *Cover coconut meat with water and blend. The amount of water you add will affect the thickness and creaminess of your coconut milk.*

3. *Strain out the milk through a nut milk bag, cheesecloth, or something similar. You will need to squeeze hard to remove all of the liquid.*

4. *Place leftover coconut pulp onto dehydrator trays that have silicone sheets, or are lined with parchment paper. Spread as thinly as possible.*

5. *Once fully dried, put into a dry blender and grind until you have a finely powdered flour. Store in an airtight container.*

FERAL FENNEL SEEDS

(Foeniculum vulgare)

Flavorful and easy to harvest, seeds from this feral plant are used liberally in both my cooking and in some of my favorite medicines. Pages 27 – 29 highlight how delicious feral fennel fronds are, with their feathery greens and tender stems. The bright yellow color of feral fennel flowers and pollen is another unique ingredient in the forager's kitchen, but it is the seeds that find their way most often into my cooking. I add them to ulu pancakes, tea blends, sugar coated like you get at Indian restaurants, added to ferments, soaked in alcohol, and mixed with garlic and Hawaiian chilis in venison or wild boar sausages. I distill my own hydrosols, and cups of fizzy water with a tablespoon of fennel seed hydrosol and splash of lime saved me from terrible indigestion during my second pregnancy. The photo below shows a favorite spice blend, which can either be ground up in a mortar & pestle or put into a spice grinder.

This wild spice mix includes feral fennel seeds (shown in center), homegrown coriander seeds (left), pa'akai Hawaiian sea salt (right), and peppercorns (upper right, mixed with wildcrafted Schinus molle).

HAOLE KOA SEEDS

(Leucaena leucocephala)

Can we think up of a different name for this plant already? My foraging friend David Bruce Leonard, who has been teaching about medicinal plants on the islands for many years, likes to call it Koa Malihini. This tree became a newcomer to the islands somewhere in the late 1800's and looks similar to keiki koa trees.

It is not a slow mover, having spread itself widely throughout the lowlands and lower mountain slopes on all of our inhabited islands.

Use of this plant for food is somewhat controversial. Haole koa contains a chemical called mimosene, which can cause alopecia if eaten in large quantities

Mature green seeds can be found in pods

over time. I recommend the mature green haole koa seeds be eaten in moderation, cooked twice, and that the cooking water be thrown out. As with many of our wild food plants, not much scientific attention has been given to them. Hopefully the future will see some research and development monies put into helping us further unlock some of the mysteries surrounding our wild foods. In lieu of sound science, we can look at some of the ethnobotanical references showing its use as a food. At my house we eat haole koa seeds in homemade tempeh.

HAOLE KOA TEMPEH

2 cups cooked soybeans

¼ cup cooked green haole koa seeds

¼ cup cooked Job's tears

2 Tbsp rice vinegar

Rhyzopus tempeh starter

Soak haole koa seeds for 24 hours. Discard water they were soaked in and boil in fresh water for 15 minutes. Strain, and discard cooking water. Repeat. Put the cooked, strained, and cooled soybeans, haole koa seeds, Job's tear grains and vinegar into a large bowl and mix well. Next, add Rhyzopus starter culture powder (see Resources page), and mix thoroughly. Spread mixture roughly 1" thick onto banana leaves , or 1 gallon plastic bags, and poke holes so it can breathe. Place in a warm area (85-90°) until a firm white mold has formed. This can take anywhere from 24 to 48 hours.

Haole koa tempeh incubating in perforated banana leaves.

Haole koa tempeh being sautéed. Try marinating it first, sautéing, and then adding to salads, sandwiches, or added on top of stews.

KIAWE

(Prosopis pallida)

Kiawe ain't just for barbeque! Those bean pods are an absolutely delicious and nutritious gem. More than any other plant I teach people about, it is this one that regularly leaves kama'aina sitting there with jaws dropped wide open in disbelief. Yes, they're edible! And millions of pounds of them are just falling to the ground every year, completely and utterly unloved. This tree of life can produce up to 6 harvests per year, and increasing droughts on the islands foretell there will only be more of this arid-adapted tree in the future. So, creative chefs are not limited by the ingredient, only by their culinary imaginations. It is with great gusto that I share a few ideas on how to incorporate this delicious and abundant wild food crop into your life.

Headed to the south side for a day at the beach? Keep your eyes out for kiawe, as it grows on the leeward sides of all our inhabited islands. Tough and hearty in arid conditions, it is

Kiawe bean pods. Photo Courtesy of Vince Kana'i Dodge

Kiawe grows on the leeward side of all Hawaiian Islands. Photo Courtesy of Vince Kana'i Dodge

remarkably salt-tolerant and can be seen growing right up to the shoreline. You can also find it popping up right out of old lava flows, and growing at up to 2000' in elevation.

Kiawe arrived in 1828 courtesy of Father Alexis Bachelot, a Jesuit who was a member of the Congregation of the Sacred Hearts of Jesus and Mary of the Perpetual Adoration of the Most Holy Sacrament of the Altar. Bachelot's boat left France in 1826, stopping off for some time in Peru. He was introduced in Peru to what the locals referred to as huarango in Quechua, and algarroba in Spanish. Its pods created a curiously delicious flour, and grapes were also grown and intercropped with the tree. Neil Logan hypothesizes that Father Bachelot must have become enamored with the local version of those holy sacraments of the Catholic faith, bread and wine, and carried the tree with him on the long journey to Hawai'i. There is a memorial plaque at the old Catholic Mission on Fort Street in Honolulu which commemorates the very first tree planted by Father Bachelot. The stump of that old grandmother tree can still be seen today.

Algarobba became kiawe in Hawai'i. The Hawaiian translation means 'a pillar' or 'to sway'. The oldest name our human family remembers for kiawe is taco, which comes from the Aymara language, and means 'the tree' or 'the one'. Neil Logan, of Integrated Living Systems Design on the Big Island, has dedicated years to researching kiawe. He turned me on to using a UV flashlight when I go out harvesting. Why? The pods can have aflatoxin, a mold that is harmful to our health, and a quick look with a UV flashlight can help you spot it. Mold can also be avoided by removing moisture from pods by drying them until they snap easily. Harvest pods as soon as they've turned yellow, and pick them directly from the tree, which will also help with mold and the bug factor. You might notice some pods have holes in them. Those holes come from bruchid beetles, and although it is ideal to avoid them, there's no harm if you eat some. So, after checking for aflatoxin, and chewing on a pod to see if I like the taste of that particular tree's bounty, I harvest. Typically, the pods are put into 5-gallon buckets and once returning home, I lay them out on tarps to dry fully in the hot sun. This can take a few days, but your diligence will pay off. If they are not fully dried they will mold, and the bruchid beetles may hatch and infest your harvest. Once crispy dry, store the harvest in airtight buckets with lids, or in ziploc baggies in the freezer.

When I get home from harvesting I look forward to a cold cup of Kiawe Cooler, and brewing a plain tea is simply delightful as well. I break the pods into roughly 2" pieces, sometimes giving them a quick pound in my mortar & pestle, cover with rainwater, and can simmer them from there. This is the base of many wonderful things. I add veggies and bones to make nourishing broth, with chicken bone and mesquite pod broth a favorite at my house. The simmered pods can also be strained and drunk as is, or boiled down into syrup. To make roughly one quart of syrup you will need 6 cups of strained pod tea and 2 cups of honey (3 parts water, 1 part honey), which is cooked down until one quart remains.

KIAWE COOLER

4 cups kiawe pods, broken into 2" pieces

10 cups water

2 Tbsp lemon or orange rind

6 wild cinnamon leaves

6 wild allspice leaves

kiawe honey to taste

Wash kiawe pods. Break pods into pieces. Place broken pods, water, and citrus rind into pot to soak overnight (roughly 8 hours). Place this mixture into a pot and put on the lowest heat setting, adding wild cinnamon and wild allspice leaves, and make sure the mixture does not boil. Simmer for an hour and a half and strain. Add honey to taste. Cool in refrigerator before serving. Garnish with a twist of lemon or orange.

Kiawe flowers are adored by bees. When they feast on the nectar of kiawe flowers it makes for some outstanding honey. I like to use kiawe honey in my Kiawe Cooler recipe, but of course any honey can be used. I would encourage you to make friends with a beekeeper on your island, or begin the fascinating journey into creating your own apiary. The Big Island of Hawai'i is home to a rare treat in the world of gourmet honey. Rare Hawaiian pure white kiawe honey that is creamy and floral is now part of the Slow Food Ark of Taste. Although kiawe honey is the main sweetener in my home, it is flour made from grinding up the entire pods that has become a true staple.

Kiawe pods are ground up whole to make kiawe flour. It has a distinct sweetness that comes from the mesocarp, a layer of pulp found between the seeds. Although often compared to carob, it has its own unique flavor and contains volatile oils that contribute to the rich chocolate and coconut-like aroma. It is difficult to make this flour in your own home, as it can bind up even the strongest of blenders and be a slow process. So, this is where I turn to Vince Dodge of Wai'anae Gold on Oahu. His business is now pumping out gorgeous kiawe flour with the help of a hammermill. This is truly a great blessing to the islands, as this flour was not available before July 2013.

---

www.waianaegold.com

Interested in ordering some locally milled kiawe flour? Check out Wai'anae Gold for their flour, 'Aina Bars and other handmade artisan creations.

Kiawe flour contains no gluten, so it is often mixed with other flours. In taste panel tests the optimum kiawe concentrations were 5% in crackers, 10% in bread, 13% in pancakes/waffles, 20% in tortillas, and 50% in chapatti (45). I tend to go with much heavier amounts in my personal use of kiawe, but it's fun to get an idea of how average Americans accept its flavor. There are ways to use kiawe that don't require other flours, like simply making crepes from kiawe flour and eggs, or a kiawe crumble. Try adding the flour to your homemade granola, coconut puddings, hot chocolate, pinole, or to coconut flour cake cooked in a solar oven!

We can get inspiration from all sorts of places when bringing kiawe into our life, as ancient cultures have been using it for generations. Several species of *Prosopis*, known as mesquite, are found in Arizona, New Mexico and Texas. I was introduced to mesquite in 2007, and met Brad Lancaster of Desert Harvesters in Tucson, AZ. That organization now has a cookbook, and travels to local communities in the desert southwest to mill pods that people have collected themselves. They have Mesquite Pancake Chow Downs during milling events that beautifully build community around wild food. I dream of having a traveling hammermill with Kiawe Cookoffs held here on the islands.

Prosopis pallida is the species of mesquite found here in Hawai'i. It originates from the dry areas of southern Peru, where the Nazca civilization flourished. It's a backbone species of the environment and culture there, but populations have been severely wiped out and it's estimated that only 1% of their kiawe forests remain. There are now major efforts to propagate the tree and repopulate it, a revival that is coming just in the nick of time.

Check out a beautiful short film titled, 'The King of the Desert is Dying', which documents a 1,074 year old kiawe tree. http://youtu.be/BqW5zF-_Lp4

Nazca lines can be seen from space, and are the creations of the ancient Nazca culture. This is from where kiawe (Prosopis pallida) originates.

AÑO WICHI

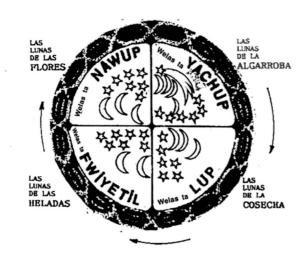

Wichi' Calendar. Photo Courtesy of the Wichi' People

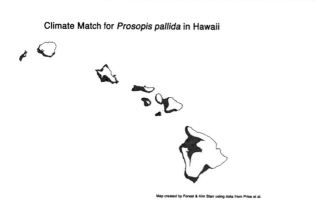

Climate Match for *Prosopis pallida* in Hawaii

Map created by Forest & Kim Starr using data from Price et al.

Areas in red show where we can find kiawe growing in the state. Image Courtesy of Forest and Kim Starr

Prosopis pallida is dwindling in its native southern Peru, but has spread to other areas in South America. It is the Wichi' people who predominantly use algorroba (kiawe) today. Their calendar shows how prominently algarroba figures into the Wichi's great turn of the seasons in their yearly calendar. Neil Logan on the Big Island, who has done much research into kiawe and traveled to their communities, reports that Wichi eat the flour in raw preparations. Recently, the eating of algarroba has gained some media attention in Argentina for its ability to feed areas struck by drought (46). As men leave home to work, women have banded together in the harvest and processing of algarroba.

Hawaii's 2050 Report says that we're looking at drought as one of the first major noticeable effects of climate change here in the Hawaiian Islands (47). The Department of Planning's 2012 Report says our state's agricultural irrigation systems are crumbling due to age (48). It seems as if we should be welcoming the gift of kiawe as an arid-adapted tree that doesn't require irrigation. The map above shows where to look for it.

'Aina Bars

A big mahalo to Vince Kana'i Dodge from Wai'anae Gold for sharing the 'Aina Bar recipe with us. These bars are a family favorite and provide a wonderful foundation from which to play. Experiment with adding wild greens superfood powder, cacao powder, purslane seeds, dehydrated starfruit, or dehydrated grated coconut.

'AINA BARS

2 parts kiawe flour

2 parts nut butter

1 part raw unheated honey

Directions

Mash all ingredients with fork until clumps are gone.

Lomi (massage) with hands until well mixed.

Refrigerate. After it has cooled remove from refrigerator and pat down with

your hands until flat. Return to refrigerator, or cold storage.

RAW KIAWE PIE CRUST

(makes 2 crusts)

1 cup kiawe flour

1 cup macadamia nuts, finely chopped

¼ cup coconut oil

1/8 cup raw honey

2 tsp macadamia nut butter

Lomi (massage) all ingredients thoroughly in a mixing bowl. Place into pie plates and spread. If mixture is too sticky to spread, place into refrigerator and try again after it has chilled.

KIAWE PODS, *with their high sugar content, ferment easily into alcoholic drinks.*

THIS DELICIOUS SPARKLING FIZZY DRINK *was made with*
kiawe pods, rainwater, and kiawe honey.

KUKUI NUT

(Aleurites moluccana)

Let there be light! Like a beacon in the landscape, kukui's pale green silvery foliage is a delight to behold. I eat no more than one roasted kukui nut per day, honoring the boundary between food and medicine, but I find that so many people have heard of its laxative effect that they dismiss it as food altogether. Not many would turn down some fresh poke with inamona, so why not add it to other things? The flavor of roasted kukui is delicious, adding diversity to our diets, and connects us to the ʻaina.

I like to gather nuts that have fallen from the tree and whose thick husks have rotted away. Check for cracks in the nuts as you harvest, and then give them the float test,

submerging in water and tossing out any that rise to the surface. Next, it's time to get roasting. Roasting can be done in the oven at 350° for one hour, while sitting over a campfire, or in a solar oven. I crack them open with my macadamia nut cracker as needed, and then store any leftover crushed roasted kukui nuts in airtight containers to use later.

Inamona made with 4 roasted kukui nuts, one for each person in my family, gets pounded with salt and added to salads, or whatever needs some nutty flavor that day.

Kukui nuts contain over 60% oil, which made them perfect for burning in torches and oil lamps of old Hawaiʻi. Today, kukui oil provides us with one of the most hopeful sources of biofuel on the islands, far outshining soybean's 20% oil content (49, 50). It became our state tree in 1959, and continues to provide us with its gifts of food, medicine, and utility.

Miscellaneous

CONIFERS

(Sequoia sempervirens, Pinus radiata)

Coastal Redwood

I still can hardly believe we have redwoods growing on
Maui. These beautiful giants provide foragers with some
fantastic flavor. Keep your eyes out for tender new growth
at the end of branches. You won't need to harvest much,
as a little goes a long way. These tender young needles
are nice as a trail nibble, or add a few in your water bottle
while hiking. I bring them home and infuse them in
vinegar that's great in ulu 'potato salad'. Chopped finely

Redwood needles

and added to wild turkey stuffing, brewed into herbal tisanes or beers, or added to honey.
They can be put into the bathtub, and I love to steam distill the needles into hydrosol that
can be used for things like grapefruit rind and redwood-infused mochi, or fizzy drinks
with ginger syrup. What a gift to have this ancient species here!

Redwood needles infuse beautifully in vinegar.

Monterey Pine

This pine tree provides us with wonderful needles to play with, in all the same ways as our redwood needles. But, they also have small pine nuts and pollen to forage as well. I have never timed my trek up the mountain correctly to harvest either of those two, but it keeps life full of exciting things on my to-do list. The following recipe goes great in 'adult' hot chocolate, especially when sitting by a fireplace on a chilly night in Kula.

PINE NEEDLE ELIXIR

1/3 honey

1/3 young pine needles, chopped

1/3 okolehao

Fill a jar 1/3 of the way with some local raw honey. Make sure your jar and pine needles do not have any moisture, as that could cause some fermentation. Chop pine needles finely and mix into honey with a spoon or chopstick. To this, add a bit of okolehao and mix some more (brandy or rum work nicely as well). Top off with more okolehao and cover. Let sit for a few weeks, giving it a shake when you think of it, then strain out needles.

SEA LETTUCE

(Ulva fasciata)

Limu palahalaha is the Hawaiian name for this sea vegetables that can be found clinging onto rocks in the intertidal zone, floating freely in the water, or washed up on the beach. Look for its bright green color and papery thin texture. Sea turtles and random foragers can be seen munching it on shorelines around Hawai'i. If you don't find fresh sea lettuce on the beach or floating in the water, you can use a pair of scissors to cut it cleanly from its holdfast. Don't tear it off the rocks!

Adding diversity to our diets, it continues to be studied for health promoting properties (51, 52). Sea lettuce can be found nearly worldwide, and is considered an invasive in many areas. You must be mindful to harvest this limu from clean waters, as it can bioaccumulate toxins and thrives in the runoff from agricultural areas using chemical fertilizers.

Sea lettuce can be eaten raw in salads, cooked into soups, put into risotto, mixed with other stronger-tasting limu, or dried into sheets similar to nori paper. Gorilla ogo (Gracilaria salicornia) is another more invasive limu and besides being eaten raw or cooked, is famous for the creation of jelly-like agar. Interested in helping bring back the gardens of sea vegetables that once contained great diversity here in the islands? Contact the Waihe'e Limu Restoration Project on Maui to get involved.

Sea lettuce in front, marsh samphire middle, and ogo in back.

Sea lettuce salad.

SEA LETTUCE SALAD

2 cups sea lettuce, cut into bite sized pieces

1 small carrot, julienned

2 Tbsp green onion, sliced

1 ½ Tbsp shoyu

1 tsp toasted sesame oil

1 Tbsp rice vinegar

1 medium-sized garlic clove, smashed and minced

1 tsp fresh ginger root, grated finely

Hawaiian chili to taste

1 roasted kukui nut, chopped finely

1 tsp sesame seeds

Thoroughly clean sea lettuce. Squeeze it dry and cut into bite sized pieces. Julienne carrots, chop green onion, and add to sea lettuce. In small bowl mix remaining ingredients. Combine all ingredients, except kukui nut and sesame seeds, and let flavors blend for an hour in refrigerator. Garnish with roasted kukui nut and sesame seeds before serving.

WILD ALLSPICE

(Pimenta dioica)

It's not hard to imagine reggae tunes blasting and some jerk chicken on the barbecue...somewhere at a beach in Hawai'i. Of course, when I barbecue it has to be wild! Allspice is one of the key ingredients in making jerk seasoning. Hailing from Jamaica, this tropical evergreen can get up to 40' tall and can now be found in Hawai'i.

Photo Courtesy of Forest & Kim Starr

It's in the Myrtle Family (Myrtaceae), which has quite a few edible relatives on the islands. Thick glossy leaves are aromatic and can be used liberally when cooking meats, vegetables, or sweets. I like to make strong brews of herbal tea with them as well, with a flavor that seems to combine clove, cinnamon, nutmeg and peppercorns all in one. They're similar to a bay leaf in that you put the whole leaf in while cooking, and remove it before serving. Unlike bay, they do not hold their aroma when dried. Unripe mature fruit are dried and ground up into a powdered spice, and it is that spice which is called for in jerk recipes and pumpkin pie. Ripe fruit are great for infusing into liquor, and the wood can also be used to smoke foods.

Photo Courtesy of Forest & Kim Starr

Healthy young allspice leaves.

127

HONEY IS A FABULOUS WAY OF PRESERVING FOODS.

On the left is honey with wild allspice leaves, center is honey with passionfruit flowers, and right is a wild basil and Maui vanilla bean honey. To make, half the jar is filled with torn pieces of the wild basil and honey is stirred in. Two vanilla beans are cut in half with seeds and beans added. Keep adding honey and torn wild basil leaves until you reach the top.

WILD BASIL

(Ocimum gratissimum)

Last year I took a trip out to Maui's wild side near Kaupo. Amidst the grasses and haole koa I saw what looked to be a member of the Mint Family (Lamiaceae). I picked one of its leaves, crushed it in my hands, and knew I had hit an aromatic treasure. This clove-smelling plant has been used widely in Africa and India for food and medicine. It continues to prove itself as a nutritional powerhouse, rich in phytonutrients (53, 54). I like to chiffonade it and add to pad thai or biriyani. It's excellent preserved in honey with vanilla beans (previous page), and those sugary leaves can be added to baked goods. It can be brewed as an herbal tea fresh or dried.

Wild basil with dried seedpods. Photo Courtesy of Forest & Kim Starr

WILD CINNAMON

(Cinnamomum burmannii)

This tree has naturalized on nearly all our inhabited islands. Although it is not true cinnamon, its inner bark and leaves are aromatic and similar in flavor. Try adding the leaves to sauces and stews when cooking, or brewing them into coffee or hot chocolate. It can be used basically the same ways that wild allspice leaves are used, and should be removed before serving to eat. They are a natural food preservative and can help the home food processor or small food business add safety to their prepared foods (55). Even in small amounts, this adds that all-important diversity (56, 57).

Wild cinnamon new leaf growth. Photo Courtesy of Forest & Kim Starr

WILD GINGER RHIZOMES

(Hedychium flavescens, H. coronarium)

There are many different kinds of ginger found in Hawai'i, and the Zingiberaceae Family is quite safe to experiment with, but I have only used the rhizomes of our yellow and white butterfly gingers. These wild ginger rhizomes have a different taste from cultivated ginger, but can be used in similar ways and add some diversity to the diet. White butterfly ginger (*Hedychium coronarium*) is a significant food and medicine crop brought to market in northeastern India (58).

I use a microplane to include small amounts of these rhizomes in my vegetable ferments, fermented fizzy drinks, and in dipping sauces for rice paper rolls and dumplings. They are used when cooking chutneys, or when making juices like guava. They can be boiled with sugar or honey into a syrup, or made into candies. Those candies can be cut up and added to cakes, or minced finely and put into coconut macaroons, or kiawe 'aina bars. The leftover sugar can be crushed and used to coat the rims of martini glasses, or just as a delicious nibble on their own. My secret ingredient is the addition of root beer flavored false awa (*Piper auritum*) flowers.

Candied false awa flowers.

Candied yellow butterfly ginger rhizomes

CANDIED WILD GINGER

Wild Ginger Rhizomes, sliced thinly

Cultivated Ginger Rhizomes, sliced thinly

False Awa Flowers, whole

Rainwater

Organic Cane Sugar

Cut away all the outside fibers of the wild ginger rhizomes, using only the tender inner portions. Slice as thinly as you can using a mandoline. Measure your sliced ginger, I use half wild and half cultivated ginger root, and false awa flowers using a 3:1 ratio, i.e. 3 cups sliced ginger to 1 cup false awa flowers. Put gingers into a pot and add roughly 4 times as much water as your combined ginger and false awa flowers mix, i.e. 4 cups combined mix and 4 cups water. Simmer for 30 minutes, until ginger becomes tender. Add false awa flowers and cook for another 2 minutes covered. Remove from heat and save a quarter of your cooking water, measuring it so you know exactly how much you have. Use another measuring cup and measure an equal amount of sugar as you have cooking water. Dump any remaining cooking water and put ginger, false awa, cooking water and sugar into a pot and cook on medium heat, stirring constantly, until the mixture begins to crystallize and look dry. Remove immediately from heat and spread out the individual pieces on a cooling rack so they don't stick together. Once dried, store in an airtight container.

WILD DRINKS

Herbal Teas

The ritual magic of bringing water together with earth (plants), through the help of fire, has been done by cultures around the planet. Even if we aren't trained in the Way of Tea ceremony, we can still be mindful of how our hands move as we hold the cup, the way in which we lift our cups to breathe in its aromatic steam, thoughts we hold close and those we let the steam carry away. Many a plant enters my teacup, bringing warmth and gentle nourishment into day-to-day life, and that teacup has witnessed both joys and sorrows. The growing of tea is seeing a revival among Hawaii's farmers, with some fabulous local black and green teas now available, but what I speak of here is herbal tea. These are also called tisanes, and if the plant material is allowed to steep for some time (think overnight) then they become decoctions. The plants cell walls are opened by water, and their nutritive and aromatic properties infuse into that water. Sometimes sweetened, sometimes drunk with cream or nut milks, and sometimes all by their delicious selves.

Teas can be brewed from dried or fresh flowers, dried or fresh fruits, seeds, peels, and roots. Leaves of wild alpine strawberry (*Fragaria vesca*) have made it into my teacup, Job's tears (*Coix lachryma-jobi*) leaves when used in quantity add a grassy sweetness, and mamaki (*Pipturus albidus*) is a favorite nutritive tea in the Nettle Family (Urticaceae). Are you suffering from diabetes or interested in preventing it? Try a tea of Spanish needles leaf to stimulate insulin secretion and improve glucose tolerance (59). Try adding some ginger, orange rind, dried starfruit, and crushed wild fennel seeds. Or try a blend of wild allspice leaves, wild cinnamon leaves, wild basil leaves, wild and cultivated ginger rhizome, cardomom, Hawaiian-grown black tea and coconut milk, for a wild version of chai.

Thimbleberry leaves make a mellow tea, and will stay fresh if placed into a jar of water.

How about a thermos of tea on your next waterfall hike? Keep your eyes out for Job's tears along the way.

COFFEE

(Coffea arabica)

Large stands of feral coffee can be found growing in wet shady areas throughout the islands. Both the leaves and fruits, known as coffee cherries, can be brewed into herbal tea with more antioxidants than regular tea (60). Share your ho'okipa, which means hospitality in Hawaiian, with cups of kope made from wild beans you have fermented, roasted, and brewed.

Leaves, cherries, and seeds can all be brewed into a hot beverage.

WILD ESPRESSO *can be embellished with syrups made from wild food plants, or hydrosols distilled from those plants, increasing diversity in the diet.*

ALCOHOLIC DRINKS

I love a good party! There have been some truly wild combinations of mixed drinks pumped out of my kitchen throughout the years, with each year and season bringing about a new set of experiments. Locally brewed vodka, rum, okolehao, and wine give the mixologist plenty of places to begin playing. I would encourage you to start by steeping wild ingredients, one at a time, in small bottles of alcohol for a few weeks, shaking regularly. Flavors of aromatic seeds, roots, flowers and fruits can all be mixed together later, once you have a good grasp of the amounts needed to create the flavor you want. Shrubs, switchels, oxymels, and elixirs are other great ways to utilize our wild food plants, along with the infusion of wild food flavors into simple syrups which are needed for so many cocktails. Popsicles with wild juices and flavors, ice cubes with wild edible flowers, or poha and hill

berries frozen on a stick, can electrify drinks. Additions like feral fennel flowers in martinis, or feral parsley fronds with oxalis and purslane greens atop a Bloody Mary, are sure to bring a squeal of delight. Poached wild fruits can be blended to make dirty martinis, or glasses rimmed with sugar colored from edible wild flowers. See pages 45 – 46 for info on making your own wild bitters, or page 83 for wild berry-infused vodka.

MANY OF THE WILD FOODS IN THIS BOOK, *when infused into*
alcohol, bring much merriment and good health when consumed in moderation. Celebrate. Enjoy life.
Here's a toast to your wild health!

RESOURCES

Starr Environmental – Plants of Hawaii

www.starrenvironmental.com/images/?o=plants

The mega-talented botanist duo Forest and Kim Starr have gifted us with this incredible website to view plants found in the islands (along with insects and birds).

Smithsonian – Flora of the Hawaiian Islands

www.botany.si.edu/pacificislandbiodiversity/hawaiianflora/query.cfm

Although I have foraged on islands other than Maui, it was this comprehensive resource that enabled me to list where the plants in this book can be found.

Medicine at Your Feet: Healing Plants of the Hawaiian Kingdom

www.earthmedicineinstitute.com

David Bruce Leonard has been working with medicinal plants, and teaching about them, for years. His book is an excellent resource for learning medicinal, and some food uses, of wild plants.

Eat The Weeds

www.eattheweeds.com

Green Deane's website is a fabulous resource, providing in-depth writing, a list of foraging instructors, and an excellent wild food forum. He lives in Florida, so many of the plants he covers can also be found in Hawai'i.

Botany in a Day

www.hollowtop.com

Thomas J. Elpel created a masterpiece that helps you gain a way of learning about plants by what family they belong to. Essential botany builder.

Euell Gibbons' Beachcombers Handbook

Published in 1967, this classic book by Euell Gibbons is the only other book dedicated to foraging in the Hawaiian Islands.

Cultures for Health

www.culturesforhealth.com

The tempeh and cheese photographed in this book were made using starters from this company.

BIBLIOGRAPHY

1. Zareen Bharucha. 2010. "The Roles and Values of Wild Foods in Agricultural Systems." *Philosophical Transactions of the Royal Society B: Biological Sciences* 365 (1554): 2913–26.

2. Harrison, Gail G. 2010. "Public Health Interventions to Combat Micronutrient Deficiencies." *Public Health Reviews (2107-6952)* 32 (1): 256–66.

3. Powell, Bronwen, Patrick Maundu, Harriet V. Kuhnlein, and Timothy Johns. 2013. "Wild Foods from Farm and Forest in the East Usambara Mountains, Tanzania." *Ecology of Food and Nutrition* 52 (6): 451–78. doi:10.1080/03670244.2013.768122

4. Senguttuvan, Jamuna, Subramaniam Paulsamy, and Krishnamoorthy Karthika. 2014. "Phytochemical Analysis and Evaluation of Leaf and Root Parts of the Medicinal Herb, *Hypochaeris radicata* L. for in Vitro Antioxidant Activities." *Asian Pacific Journal of Tropical Biomedicine* 4 (Suppl 1): S359–67. doi:10.12980/APJTB.4.2014C1030

5. Trichopoulou A, Vasilopoulou E, Hollman P, Chamalides CH, Foufa E. 2000. "Nutritional composition and flavonoid content of edible wild greens and green pies: a potential rich source of antioxidant nutrients in the Mediterranean diet." *Food Chemistry* 70(3): 319-323. doi: 10.1016/S0308-8146(00)00091-1

6. Mona T. M Ghanem, Hany M.A. Radwan, El-Sayed Mahdy M., Yehya M. Elkholy, Heba D. Hassanein, and Abdelaaty A. Shahat. 2012. "Phenolic Compounds from Foeniculum Vulgare (Subsp. Piperitum) (Apiaceae) Herb and Evaluation of Hepatoprotective Antioxidant Activity." *Pharmacognosy Research* 4(2): 104–108. doi:10.4103/0974-8490.94735

7. Mahmood, Sidra, Shahzad Hussain, and Farnaz Malik. 2014. "Critique of Medicinal Conspicuousness of Parsley (*Petroselinum crispum*): A Culinary Herb of Mediterranean Region." *Pakistan Journal of Pharmaceutical Sciences* 27 (1): 193–202.

8. Veerendra Kumar, M. H, and Y. K Gupta. 2002. "Effect of Different Extracts of *Centella asiatica* on Cognition and Markers of Oxidative Stress in Rats." *Journal of Ethnopharmacology* 79 (2): 253–60. doi:10.1016/S0378-8741(01)00394-4

9. Zainol, M. K, A Abd-Hamid, S Yusof, and R Muse. 2003. "Antioxidative Activity and Total Phenolic Compounds of Leaf, Root and Petiole of Four Accessions of *Centella asiatica* (L.) Urban." *Food Chemistry* 81 (4): 575–81. doi:10.1016/S0308-8146(02)00498-3

10. Yousif, Basim S., Liu, L.Y., Masaoka, Y., Saneoka, H. 2010. "Comparative Studies in Salinity Tolerance Between New Zealand Spinach (*Tetragonia tetragonioides*) and Chard (*Beta vulgaris*) to Salt Stress." *Agricultural Journal* 5(1): 19-24.

11. Jain, A., Sundriyal M., Roshnibala, S., Kotoky, R., Kanjilal P.B., Singh, H.B., Sundriyal, R.C. 2011. "Dietary Use and Conservation Concern of Edible Wetland Plants at Indo-Burma Hotspot: a Case Study From Northeast India." *Journal of Ethnobiology and Ethnomedicine* 7:29. doi:10.1186/1746-4269-7-29

12. Saikia, Pankaj, and Dibakar Chandra Deka. 2013. "Mineral Content of Some Wild Green Leafy Vegetables of North-East India." *Journal of Chemical & Pharmaceutical Research* 5 (3): 117–21.

13. Alam, Md. Amirul, Abdul Shukor Juraimi, M. Y. Rafii, Azizah Abdul Hamid, and Farzad Aslani. 2014. "Screening of Purslane (*Portulaca oleracea* L.) Accessions for High Salt Tolerance." *The Scientific World Journal* 2014. doi:10.1155/2014/627916

14. Aberoumand, Ali. 2009. "Nutritional Evaluation of Edible *Portulaca oleracea* as Plant Food." *Food Analytical Methods* 2 (3): 204–7. doi:10.1007/s12161-008-9049-9

15. Uddin, Md. Kamal, Abdul Shukor Juraimi, Md Sabir Hossain, Most. Altaf Un Nahar, Md. Eaqub Ali, and M. M. Rahman. 2014. "Purslane Weed (*Portulaca oleracea*): A Prospective Plant Source of Nutrition, Omega-3 Fatty Acid, and Antioxidant Attributes." *The Scientific World Journal* 2014 (February). doi:10.1155/2014/951019

16. McDowell, Arlene, Scott Thompson, Mirjam Stark, Zong-Quan Ou, and Kevin S. Gould. 2011. "Antioxidant Activity of Puha (*Sonchus oleraceus* L.) as Assessed by the Cellular Antioxidant Activity (CAA) Assay." *Phytotherapy Research* 25 (12): 1876–82. doi:10.1002/ptr.3648

17. Ou, Zong-Quan, David M. Schmierer, Clare J. Strachan, Thomas Rades, and Arlene McDowell. 2014. "Influence of Postharvest Processing and Storage Conditions on Key Antioxidants in Puha (*Sonchus oleraceus* L.)." *The Journal of Pharmacy and Pharmacology* 66 (7): 998–1008. doi:10.1111/jphp.12220

18. Chipurura, Batsirai, Maud Muchuweti, and Abisha Kasiyamhuru. 2013. "Wild Leafy Vegetables Consumed in Buhera District of Zimbabwe and Their Phenolic Compounds Content." *Ecology of Food and Nutrition* 52 (2): 178–89. doi:10.1080/03670 244.2012.706094

19. Pablo Rodríguez, Elevina Pérez. 2011. "Characterization of the Proteins Fractions Extracted from Leaves of *Amaranthus dubius* (*Amaranthus Spp.*)." *African Journal of Food Science* 5: 417–24.

20. Akubugwo, I. E., Obasi, N. A., Chinyere G. C. and Ugbogu A. E. 2007. "Nutritional and chemical value of *Amaranthus hybridus* L. leaves from Afikpo, Nigeria." *African Journal of Biotechnology* Vol. 6 (24), pp. 2833-2839. doi:10.5897/AJB2007.000-2452

21. Barminas, J. T., Milam Charles, and D. Emmanuel. 1998. "Mineral Composition of Non-Conventional Leafy Vegetables." *Plant Foods for Human Nutrition* 53 (1): 29–36. doi:10.1023/A:1008084007189

22. Odom T.C, Udensi E.A., and Iwe M.O. 2013. "Nutritional Evaluation of Unripe Carica Papaya Unripe Musa paradisiacal and Mucuna Cochichinensis, Weaning Food Formulation." *European Journal Biology and Medical Science.* 1 (1): 6-15.

23. Ekesa, Beatrice, Marie Poulaert, Mark W. Davey, Judith Kimiywe, Inge Van den Bergh, Guy Blomme, and Claudie Dhuique-Mayer. 2012. "Bioaccessibility of Provitamin A Carotenoids in Bananas (*Musa Spp.*) and Derived Dishes in African Countries." *Food Chemistry*, Advances in Potato Chemistry, Nutrition and Technology, 133 (4): 1471–77. doi:10.1016/j.foodchem.2012.02.036

24. Chandrika, U. G., K. S. S. P. Fernando, and K. K. D. S. Ranaweera. 2009. "Carotenoid Content and in Vitro Bioaccessibility of Lycopene from Guava (*Psidium guajava*) and Watermelon (*Citrullus lanatus*) by High-Performance Liquid Chromatography Diode Array Detection." *International Journal of Food Sciences and Nutrition* 60 (7): 558–66. doi:10.3109/09637480801987195

25. Ribeiro, Alessandra Braga, Renan Campos Chisté, Marisa Freitas, Alex Fiori da Silva, Jesuí Vergílio Visentainer, and Eduarda Fernandes. 2014. "*Psidium cattleianum* Fruit Extracts Are Efficient in Vitro Scavengers of Physiologically Relevant Reactive Oxygen and Nitrogen Species." *Food Chemistry* 165 (December): 140–48. doi:10.1016/j.foodchem.2014.05.079

26. McCook-Russell, Kayanne P., Muraleedharan G. Nair, Petrea C. Facey, and Camille S. Bowen-Forbes. 2012. "Nutritional and Nutraceutical Comparison of Jamaican *Psidium cattleianum* (strawberry Guava) and *Psidium guajava* (common Guava) Fruits." *Food Chemistry* 134 (2): 1069–73. doi:10.1016/j.foodchem.2012.03.018

27. Ordóñez-Santos, Luís E., and Andrea Vázquez-Riascos. 2010. "Effect of Processing and Storage Time on the Vitamin C and Lycopene Contents of Nectar of Pink Guava (*Psidium guajava* L.)." *Archivos Latinoamericanos De Nutrición* 60 (3): 280–84.

28. Ramya, S., Neethirajan, K., Jayakumararaj, R. 2012. "Profile of bioactive compounds in *Syzygium cumini* -- a review." *Journal of Pharmacy Research* 5 (8): 4548.

29. Rufino, Maria S. M., Alves, Ricardo E., Brito, Edy S., Pérez-Jiménez, Jara, Saura-Calixto, Fulgencio, and Mancini-Filho, Jorge. 2010. "Bioactive compounds and antioxidant capacities of 18 non-traditional tropical fruits from Brazil" *Food Chemistry*. 121: 996–1002.

30. Atale, Neha, Khushboo Gupta, and Vibha Rani. 2014. "Protective Effect of *Syzygium cumini* against Pesticide-Induced Cardiotoxicity." *Environmental Science and Pollution Research* 21 (13): 7956–72. doi:10.1007/s11356-014-2684-3

31. Moodley, Roshila, Hafizah Chenia, Sreekanth B. Jonnalagadda, and Neil Koorbanally. 2011. "Antibacterial and Anti-Adhesion Activity of the Pentacyclic Triterpenoids Isolated from the Leaves and Edible Fruits of *Carissa macrocarpa*." *Journal of Medicinal Plants Research* 5 (19): 4851–58.

32. Bravo, Karent, Stella Sepulveda-Ortega, Oscar Lara-Guzman, Alejandro A. Navas-Arboleda, and Edison Osorio. 2014. "Influence of Cultivar and Ripening Time on Bioactive Compounds and Antioxidant Properties in Cape Gooseberry (*Physalis peruviana* L.)." *Journal of the Science of Food and Agriculture*, August. doi:10.1002/jsfa.6866.

33. Puente, Luis A., Claudia A. Pinto-Muñoz, Eduardo S. Castro, and Misael Cortes. 2011. *Food Research International* 44: 1733–1740.

34. Yilmaztekin, Murat. 2014. "Analysis of Volatile Components of Cape Gooseberry (*Physalis peruviana* L.) Grown in Turkey by HS-SPME and GC-MS." *The Scientific World Journal*. March. doi:10.1155/2014/796097

35. Al-Olayan, Ebitisam M., Manal F. El-Khadragy, Ahmed M. Aref, Mohamed S. Othman, Rami B. Kassab, and Ahmed E.A. Moneim. 2014. "The Potential Protective Effect of *Physalis peruviana* L. against Carbon Tetrachloride-Induced Hepatotoxicity in Rats Is Mediated by Suppression of Oxidative Stress and Downregulation of MMP-9 Expression." *Oxidative Medicine and Cellular Longevity*. 2014: 381413. doi:10.1155/2014/381413

36. López-Romero, Patricia, Edgar Pichardo-Ontiveros, Azalia Avila-Nava, Natalia Vázquez-Manjarrez, Armando R. Tovar, José Pedraza-Chaverri, and Nimbe Torres. 2014. "The Effect of Nopal (*Opuntia ficus indica*) on Postprandial Blood Glucose, Incretins, and Antioxidant Activity in Mexican Patients with Type 2 Diabetes after Consumption of Two Different Composition Breakfasts." *Journal of the Academy of Nutrition and Dietetics* 114 (11): 1811–18. doi:10.1016/j.jand.2014.06.352

37. Harris, Cory S., Alain Cuerrier, Erin Lamont, Pierre S. Haddad, John T. Arnason, Steffany A. L. Bennett, and Timothy Johns. 2014. "Investigating Wild Berries as a Dietary Approach to Reducing the Formation of Advanced Glycation Endproducts: Chemical Correlates of in Vitro Antiglycation Activity." *Plant Foods for Human Nutrition (Dordrecht, Netherlands)* 69 (1): 71–77. doi:10.1007/s11130-014-0403-3

38. "Rubus niveus f. b." Starr Environmental report, accessed on December 29, 2014, http://www.starrenvironmental.com/publications/species_reports/pdf/rubus_niveus_f_b.pdf.

39. Bowen-Forbes, Camille S., Vanisree Mulabagal, Yunbao Liu, and Muraleedharan G. Nair. 2009. "Ursolic Acid Analogues: Non-Phenolic Functional Food Components in Jamaican Raspberry Fruits." *Food Chemistry* 116 (3): 633–37. doi:10.1016/j.foodchem.2009.02.075.

40. Rosa, Renato Moreira, Maria Inés S. Melecchi, Fernanda C. Abad, Cristina Rosat Simoni, Elina B. Caramão, João Antonio Pêgas Henriques, Jenifer Saffi, and Ana Lígia Lia de Paula Ramos. 2006. "Antioxidant and Antimutagenic Properties of *Hibiscus tiliaceus* L. Methanolic Extract." *Journal of Agricultural and Food Chemistry* 54 (19): 7324–30. doi:10.1021/jf061407b

41. Garzon, G.A. and Wrolstad, R. E. 2008. "Major anthocyanins and antioxidant activity of Nasturtium flowers (*Tropaeolum majus*)." *Food Chemistry* 114 (1): 44–49. doi:10.1016/j.foodchem.2008.09.013

42. Niizu, P.Y. and Delia B. Rodriguez-Amaya. 2005. "Flowers and Leaves of *Tropaeolum majus* L. as Rich Sources of Lutein." *Journal of Food Science* 70(9): S605-S609.

43. Butnariu, M., and Bostan, C. "Antimicrobial and anti-inflammatory activities of the volatile oil compounds from *Tropaeolum majus* L. (Nasturtium)." *African Journal of Biotechnology*. 10(31).

44. Matos, L., Nzikou, J. M., Kimbonguila, A., Ndangui, C. B., Pambou-Tobi, N. P. G., Abena, A. A., Silou, T., Scher, J., and Desobry, S. 2009. "Composition and Nutritional Properties of Seeds and Oil from Terminalia catappa L." *Advance Journal of Food Science and Technology* 1 (1): 72 – 77.

45. Felker, Peter, Takeoka, G., and Dao, L. 2013. "Pod Mesocarp Flour of North and South American Species of Leguminous Tree Prosopis (Mesquite): Composition and Food Applications." *Food Reviews International* 29(1). doi: 10.1080/87559129.2012.692139.

46. Fabiana Frayssinet. "Seedpods Worth More than Gold in Argentina's Arid North." *TierrAmerica.* January 2, 2014.

47. Russel Kokubun, Berg, L., Chong, P., Oakland, S.C., Costa, I., Eng, H., Gabbard, M., *et al.* 2013. "Hawaii 2050: Building a Shared Future." Hawaii Sustainability Task Force. 48. Hawaii State Office of Planning in cooperation with the Hawaii Department of Agriculture. "Increased Food Security and Food Self-Sufficiency Strategy." October 2012.

49. Kibazohi, O., and R. S. Sangwan. 2011. "Vegetable Oil Production Potential from *Jatropha curcas, Croton megalocarpus, Aleurites moluccana, Moringa oleifera and Pachira glabra*: Assessment of Renewable Energy Resources for Bio-Energy Production in Africa." *Biomass and Bioenergy* 35 (3): 1352–56. doi:10.1016/j.biombioe.2010.12.048

50. Lima, José R., Fabricia Gasparini, Nadia de L. Camargo, Yussra A. Ghani, Rondenelly B. da Silva, and José E. de Oliveira. "Indian-nut (*Aleurites moluccana*) and tucum (*Astrocaryum vulgare)*, non agricultural sources for biodiesel production using ethanol: composition, characterization and optimization of the reactional production conditions." Presented at the World Renewable Energy Congress in May 2011.

51. Ryu, Min Ju, Areum Daseul Kim, Kyoung Ah Kang, Ha Sook Chung, Hye Sun Kim, In Soo Suh, Weon Young Chang, and Jin Won Hyun. 2013. "The Green Algae *Ulva fasciata* Delile Extract Induces Apoptotic Cell Death in Human Colon Cancer Cells." *In Vitro Cellular & Developmental Biology Animal* 49 (1): 74–81. doi:10.1007/s11626-012-9547-3

52. Vijayavel, Kannappan, and Jonathan A. Martinez. 2010. "In Vitro Antioxidant and Antimicrobial Activities of Two Hawaiian Marine Limu: *Ulva fasciata* (Chlorophyta) and *Gracilaria salicornia* (Rhodophyta)." *Journal of Medicinal Food* 13 (6): 1494–99. doi:10.1089/jmf.2009.0287

53. Igbinosa, Etinosa O, Edwina O Uzunuigbe, Isoken H Igbinosa, Emmanuel E Odjadjare, Nicholas O Igiehon, and Oke A Emuedo. 2013. "In Vitro Assessment of Antioxidant, Phytochemical and Nutritional Properties of Extracts from the Leaves of *Ocimum gratissimum* (Linn)." *African Journal of Traditional, Complementary, and Alternative Medicines* 10 (5): 292–98.

54. Akinmoladun AC, Ibukun EO, Emmanuel A, Obuotor EM, Farombi EO. 2007. "Phytochemical constituent and antioxidant activity of extract from the leaves of *Ocimum gratissimum*." *Scientific Research and Essay* 2: 163-6

55. Shan, Bin, Yi-Zhong Cai, John D. Brooks, and Harold Corke. 2007. "Antibacterial Properties and Major Bioactive Components of Cinnamon Stick (*Cinnamomum burmannii*): Activity against Foodborne Pathogenic Bacteria." *Journal of Agricultural and Food Chemistry* 55 (14): 5484–90. doi:10.1021/jf070424d

56. Al-Dhubiab, Bandar E. 2012. "Pharmaceutical Applications and Phytochemical Profile of *Cinnamomum burmannii*." *Pharmacognosy Reviews* 6 (12): 125–31. doi:10.4103/0973-7847.99946

57. Prasad, K. Nagendra, Bao Yang, Xinhong Dong, Guoxiang Jiang, Haiyan Zhang, Haihui Xie, and Yueming Jiang. 2009. "Flavonoid Contents and Antioxidant Activities from Cinnamomum Species." *Innovative Food Science & Emerging Technologies* 10 (4): 627–32. doi:10.1016/j.ifset.2009.05.009

58. Jain, A., M. Sundriyal, S. Roshnibala, R. Kotoky, P. B. Kanjilal, H. B. Singh, and R. C. Sundriyal. 2011. "Dietary Use and Conservation Concern of Edible Wetland Plants at Indo-Burma Hotspot: A Case Study from Northeast India." *Journal of Ethnobiology and Ethnomedicine* 7 (1): 29. doi:10.1186/1746-4269-7-29

59. Hsu, Yi-Jou, Tsung-Han Lee, Cicero Lee-Tian Chang, Yuh-Ting Huang, and Wen-Chin Yang. 2009. "Anti-Hyperglycemic Effects and Mechanism of *Bidens pilosa* Water Extract." *Journal of Ethnopharmacology* 122 (2): 379–83. doi:10.1016/j.jep.2008.12.027

60. Campa, Claudine, Laurence Mondolot, Arsene Rakotondravao, Luc P. R. Bidel, Annick Gargadennec, Emmanuel Couturon, Philippe La Fisca, Jean-Jacques Rakotomalala, Christian Jay-Allemand, and Aaron P. Davis. 2012. "A Survey of Mangiferin and Hydroxycinnamic Acid Ester Accumulation in Coffee (Coffea) Leaves: Biological Implications and Uses." *Annals of Botany*, June, mcs119. doi:10.1093/aob/mcs119

INDEX

NOTES

NOTES

NOTES

Made in the USA
San Bernardino, CA
11 March 2015